FACTION

Short Stories by 22 Film Personalities

Edited by

KHALID MOHAMED

OM

Om Books International

Published in 2013 by

OM
Om Books International

Corporate & Editorial Office
A-12, Sector 64, Noida 201 301
Uttar Pradesh, India
Phone: +91 120 477 4100
Email: editorial@ombooks.com
Website: www.ombooksinternational.com

Sales Office
4379/4B, Prakash House, Ansari Road
Darya Ganj, New Delhi 110 002, India
Phone: +91 11 2326 3363, 2326 5303
Fax: +91 11 2327 8091
Email: sales@ombooks.com
Website: www.ombooks.com

Back cover photograph of Khalid Mohamed: Subi Samuel
Photographs by Suresh Natarajan, Subi Samuel and Karan Desai
Family Fiction (p. xiv) courtesy Sudhir Patwardhan

ISBN: 978-93-81607-13-8

10 9 8 7 6 5 4 3 2 1

Printed in India

KHALID MOHAMED started as reviewer and co-editor, during his teenaged years, for *Close-Up*, a film society quarterly magazine. He then covered crime, politics and the arts for *The Times of India*, Mumbai, from the mid-1970s, engaged in daily reporting and film criticism.

Appointed Media Editor of the paper, he was next editor of *Filmfare* magazine, while continuing as the daily's film critic for 27 years. He reviewed television for *The Economic Times* besides contributing articles to *The Illustrated Weekly of India* and *Femina*. His writing has also featured in *India Today*, *The Indian Express*, *The Telegraph*, the international film weekly *Variety* and in *Sunday Observer*, London.

He was film critic for *Mid-day*, Senior Editor of *DNA* newspaper, and National Culture Editor and film critic for *Hindustan Times*. Currently, he is Consulting Editor to the *Deccan Chronicle-Asian Age* media group.

A post-graduate in Political Science from Mumbai's St Xavier's College, he has translated eminent painter MF Husain's autobiography—*Where Art Thou?*—from Hindustani to English.

He has written the original stories and screenplays for three films by Shyam Benegal: *Mammo*, *Sardari Begum* and *Zubeidaa*. He wrote the original stories and screenplays and also directed the films *Fiza*, *Tehzeeb* and *Silsiilay*.

Two years ago, he debuted as a playwright and director of the stageplay *Kennedy Bridge*. His documentary *The Last Irani Chai* has been screened widely. His second documentary *Little Big People*, on Mumbai's street children, has made news for its eye-opening portrayal of reality. Presently, he is at work on a documentary on Shyam Benegal, and his first novel.

After *Two Mothers and Other Stories*, *Faction: Short Stories by 22 Film Personalities* is his second collection.

To Fayazi Ma, who gifted me more stories than I can even try to narrate in a lifetime

CONTENTS

Photograph by Udaiveer Singh Rathore

ACKNOWLEDGEMENTS

Gautam Rajadhyaksha, my friend and Agony Uncle, is no more. Neither are quite a few support-systems who have made their exits for reasons best known to them. Like it or not, a journalist is most often judged on the scales of market equity of the moment. Others have stayed on despite my incorrigible angularities.

Heart-bracingly, though, some new ones have entered in the roles of mute cheer-leaders. I know they are there for me in all weathers, fair or foul. For *Faction: Short Stories by 22 Film Personalities,* I express my gratitude to:

Farouq Rattonsey, for checking every morning about the book's progress, or the lack of it, ending the wake-up phone call with, 'So we'll be in touch.' We are, come 8 a.m.;

Suman and Deepak Gupta, my extended family in New Delhi, who inquire, 'So when do we reserve the Pearl Jam suite for you?' That's a reference to a vintage poster of the rock band Pearl Jam, which dominates the room where I can relocate and reboot, come Dilli winter;

And their daughter, Sumi Gupta, at a 19-hours' distance in London, and a strict critic of whatever I write that I email her for comments;

Sudhir Patwardhan, an artist and a gentleman. His artworks on life in a metro have been deeply insightful and compassionate. That he permitted me to use his masterwork *Family Fiction*, in the book, without asking 'Why?' and 'Where exactly?', will be treasured as a 'wow' moment;

Chintan Upadhyay, for constantly advising me to return to Big Bollywood filmmaking. In vain. I'd rather paint a big canvas. 'Not a good idea,' he sums up, after viewing one of my Sunday afternoon abstracts;

Anwari Chaudhary, my aunt, who left me with the plea, 'I've even cleaned your bottom when you were a kid. So do something nice for me when I'm dead and gone.' I still have to fulfill her request;

Deepa Gahlot, a friend, who if not contacted for a couple of days, will dart an SMS, wondering, 'Wot? Wot?' to which she gets the same ol' answer, 'Still on the bk. Not finshd yt. (: (: (: ;

Tanuj Garg, CEO of a film production corporation, who breathes, eats and burps blockbuster movies. And he sings, too, on faint persuasion;

Bharti Garg, Tanuj's mother, who shares views on contemporary art, and just for that, sends me tiffins packed with home-cooked dinners. Vegetarian. 'Good for you,' she writes in an accompanying note;

Nilufer Qureshi, for her Dolby-sound laughter, even when I've cracked a lousy one. And for suddenly sending over a micro-oven, brand-new;

Vajir Singh, who's so sentimental that he cries, but only when I'm not looking;

Rashid Irani, who never lets me finish a sentence, preferring perhaps to read a collection of them in a book, and then nitpicks;

Rafique Baghdadi, my one-man book store, for handing over a sizeable stack whenever I quiz, 'Read anything good, lately?'

Suresh and Priya Chabria, sequestered in Pune, role-models for leading a life infused with cinema, literature, art and music.

Veenapani Chawla, away in Puducherry, who invites me there to partake of theatre workshops, and for evening traipses down memory corridors of our political philosophy days at the Mumbai University;

Anjum Rizvi, the genial film producer of *A Wednesday*, who refuses to read my script of *A Thursday*;

Ramesh Talwar of IPTA, who is astonishing in his devotion to progressive theatre;

Nupur Kapoor Nerurkar and Rajiv Nerurkar, just a doorbell away;

Indira Kapoor, for her impeccable taste and manners, and for still regarding me as the boy she first saw in knee-pants;

Sabir Masani, the protector;

Sooni Taraporevala, for free consultancy on anything to do with writing;

Firdaus Battiwala, a doctor possessing Da Vinci artistry;

Ketaki Sheth, for her onging kindness;

Manika Sharma, who calls me 'Tollo'. She believes the nickname suits me;

Shikha Trivedy, whom I've nicknamed 'Rose Petals' for her beauty;

Ayesha Kagal, once a newsroom colleague, absolutely unchanged, and chronically self-deprecatory;

Karan Desai, my assistant, who quakes when I lose it, but knows it's to make him punctual. He refuses to wear a watch;

Papia Guha, who continues to say, 'We must catch up over a cup of coffee,' although she has changed her loyalty to green tea;

Suresh Natarajan for giving me instant access to his amazing photographs;

Subi Samuel for his warmth, and warmer celebrity photographs;

And *shukriyas*, finally, to U S Rau, Behram Contractor and B Seshagiri Rao who taught me the cardinal rule of writing: always write with a beginning, middle...and end.

Family Fiction, Sudhir Patwardhan, 2010.

BACKSTORY

Quite a few moons and stars ago, in the course of a labyrinthine conversation, an actor skittered off-tangent. He zapped back to his home in Delhi where the summer's afternoon vapours would be combated by sprinkling water on the stone floors. The chore was assigned to him, a 10-year-old then, but he would rope in the gardener's frail son who ended up carrying a bucket of ice-slab water, far too heavy for him.

The gardener's son was browbeaten into believing that the cooling task was a game. A raw mango would be awarded to the one who finished first. Invariably, it would be the gardener's son.

I interrupted to point out that the anecdote had shades of Mark Twain's Tom Sawyer, the puck who conned his friends into whitewashing a fence, even feeling grateful at the end of the slog.

'I don't know about the comparison to Tom Sawyer,' the actor said almost to himself, requested me to switch off the tape-recorder and proceeded. 'This has nothing to do with our conversation today...the story just popped into my head after all these years. If you don't mind, could I complete it? Not for publication, but just to jog my memory.'

Sure.

Besides the raw mangoes, the gardener's son began to gain the empathy of the household's patriarch. 'Unwittingly, I had made him a little hero,' the narration continued. 'My father, always observant and aware of the cruel games children play with each other, began to lavish far more affection on the gardener's son than he did on his own two sons. I behaved nastily with the boy, concocted stories that he was stealing food from the kitchen, my pencils and crayons...till he was banned from entering the house. My father was upset...how could the boy he doted on do this?

'To keep his job, the gardener sent his son away. I didn't ask where or why. I was relieved that my father's affection was where it belonged. And I forgot about that boy with large eyes which had always concentrated on the stone floors. He had never dared to look at my brother or me. That would have been sheer insolence.'

If I hold back the actor's name, it's simply because he completed the story in a rush. To attach the actor's byline to a sketchy story would not be fair. I cannot ask him to complete it either, since it is difficult if not impossible to open up actors on subjects which do not fetch them instant publicity or an instant status upgrade on the reader's radar. 'That was just something I was trying to remember that day,' would be the prompt rebuff. 'It's not for public consumption.'

The banishment of the gardener's son had shades of *The Kite Runner* perhaps, but was narrated to me at least a decade and a half ago—long before Khaled Hosseini's book was published.

The actor had ended the story perfunctorily. He couldn't or didn't want to remember more, except for the epilogue. The boy who aroused a mean streak in him, is a top-rung IAS officer now, and visited the actor to say, 'Hello.' Neither spoke of that banishment; it was a cordial meeting over a cup of tea.

The story with all its ramifications—about a disadvantaged boy who made good—has stayed with me. Like so many stories I have heard *en passant* from film personalities, it will remain incomplete, the fate of so many unarticulated stories.

This collection has been motivated with the purpose of excavating stories from an eclectic cross-section of film actors and directors—stalwarts, freshers and the in-betweens. I must have interviewed most of them, but this time, the intention was to discover stories which have been dormant in the corridors of their hearts and minds. Most, as it happened, sought to relate stories attached to their own lives, their own immediate and distant experiences.

Experience—more romantically called memory—is a tremendous leveller. Or as the British art critic and writer John Berger put it, 'The movement of writing resembles that of a shuttlecock: repeatedly it approaches and withdraws, closes in and takes distance. Unlike a shuttlecock, however, it is not fixed to a static frame. As the movement of writing repeats itself…its intimacy to the experience increases. Finally, if one is fortunate, meaning is the fruit of this intimacy.'

By 'meaning', Berger, in effect, suggested that experience when prodded or re-played, results in a story. It is one way of reaching there.

As for imagination, that's a facet most actors reserve for their profession. The most competent of them draw upon 'emotional memory', linking a scene they are about to perform, to real life. For instance, I have seen an actress perform a scene of total helplessness in the situation of a communal riot so authentically that I asked her how she did it. 'Because I remember what happened on the streets during the communal riots of 1993-'94 in Bombay,' she answered. 'I saw the countless tragedies upfront. I've experienced it myself.'

Some actors, however, are content in describing themselves as 'switch-on-switch-off artistes'. They have the technical flair to identify and partake of situations absolutely alien to them, and that too—at times—with miraculous spontaneity.

Directors, too, draw from real life to write stories, novels, media commentaries and, occasionally, their own screenplays. Those who write stories and screenplays, as well as direct them, are closer to their material, which can be a good or a bad thing. The positive aspect is that they have already seen the movie—in images, sounds and milieus—unspooling on paper. The downside is that some directors are so close to the material that they cannot view the script objectively.

More often than not, directors work on screenplays written by others. 'If I am making a science-fiction movie about spaceships and extraterrestrials, where's the question of drawing from reality?' asked a director of blockbuster action movies. 'Sorry, can't think of any story for your collection,' he apologised. 'I merely execute what's given to me by the screenplay writers...after many, many discussions, of course.'

The 22 stories come under the title of *Faction* for the simple rationale, 'Never let the truth come in the way of a good story.' That kind of ornamental subversion didn't have to be applied excessively though. On the contrary, one story could not be included because the actor concluded, 'But this isn't the way it happened. The details would fill up an entire book.' Precisely. His struggle to overcome a serious illness is a book by itself—a story of the triumph of the will which just might be written by him when he is ready to recall every breath taken to combat the physical debility.

A couple of other accounts couldn't make it to the collection, purely because I could not effectively communicate the brief for a short story. In the process, I lost out on the friendship of at least two accomplished film personalities. When any semblance of discussion is *verboten,* when the writing style runs like a bull in a porcelain shop, and editorial suggestions are shot down, an impasse is unavoidable. A senior actress had handed over a story—limned with drama and tragedy—but after virtually every third paragraph, there was a sub-heading, and chapter titles too. Politely, I remarked, 'But this is not a novel, there are too many breaks.' Her instant response: 'I can start a new trend, can't I?'

There was no point arguing at our polite Emily Post-like rendezvous, punctuated by tea, sandwiches and the yelps of a frisky Chihuahua. I sought to convince her that there would be minimal editing. Smiled she, smiled I. She promised it would be waiting in the mail for me before I reached home. It wasn't.

Undaunted, a fortnight later, I made polite inquiries about its status, and perhaps politically incorrectly, pointed out that every writer, including Nobel prize winners, requires an editor's finessing. The lady hit the roof and snapped back that I wasn't a Nobel prize winner in any case. The implication was how dare I bring up the N-word? More brutally, she ended, 'You seem to want to write all the stories yourself!'

End of story.

Another actor, whom I've known ever since he was a toddler in showbiz, in the midst of performing a Bhangra-Psy-Kathak on a dance floor, grinned fluorescently at me through the strobe lights. To get the update on his story, I ventured onto the dance floor (with a boisterous partner) to check on when his email would reach me. Shaking hips, legs and what-not, I quizzed to the rhythm of a 'Mehbooba Mehbooba' remix, 'So have you started?' to be assured, 'I've started writing, been at it for quite a few days now.' This was more thrilling than bungee-jumping, till he signed off, 'I've completed five lines.' Didn't pursue him for those five lines. Not worth it. They wouldn't have fitted the format.

The format, did I say? To a degree, I did hope for a classic beginning, middle and end in the O. Henry style, and sought to work towards that. Yet, I did leave a window open, 'Make it hallucinatory, open-ended, a fantasy...anything you like,' was one of the exhortations. Not surprisingly, it didn't interest any of the contributors; it would be too vague and obtuse. The accent then was on the personal and the little-known stories from their lives—no need for any more directions here, no maps required.

'The best emotions to write out of are anger and fear or dread,' the American critic, filmmaker and political activist Susan Sontag maintained. 'The least energising emotion is to write out of admiration...because the basic feeling that goes with admiration is a passive, contemplative mood.' I would go with Sontag completely, but no impositions for the writers again. The mood and tenor were left to each individual writer to determine.

Down the years, I've seen that interviews for print and television, and now the Internet, are strictly constrained. No one opens up; the level of intimacy desired is never quite reached. Like all of us, film people keep a large part of themselves hidden. Try however hard as I have for newspaper and magazine interviews, there have been only a few insightful confessions. Like the admission by an actor that at a funeral ceremony, he ends up watching how the mourners are behaving so that he can use that in one of his performances. Another actor said that he battles with the gushing water from a power shower to see who wins. Yet another said that she didn't imitate life, but life imitated her: 'Just see the women in the brothels, they all dance and behave like me.' Quite true, actually.

Fact and fiction—or faction—is a tantalising blend, essential for the best of raconteurs. Of them all, Dilip Kumar is a marvel at this. He once confided, 'I tell stories from my youth...I describe desert stretches, camel rides and the scent of apricot pilauf with accuracy. Truth be told, I make most of the stories up.' Besides Dilip *saab*, the two unequalled story-tellers in the Mumbai film enclave, happen to be none other than Salim Khan and Javed Akhtar. They rely more on fact while recalling their days of near unemployment, but are aware that some fictional exaggeration makes their stories humorous, like Salim Khan's narration about spending two wintry nights in a cold water flat in London. He was there at the invitation of a flamboyant actor-producer-director who had fixed the writer and his wife in cheap lodgings. It was so cold there, the Khan laughs, that his wife and he had to sleep with the mattress over them, and their footwear on. Javed Akhtar's stories are more under control—particularly about his days at Mumbai's Mahakali caves where he would find shelter—but there's always a punchline which is hilariously self-deprecatory.

I did not seek to include them in *Faction:* Dilip Kumar is into his autobiography. Salim and Javed are not exactly short story writers. Javed has published collections of poems. Salim, I know, thinks only in the screenplay format, and has many incomplete ones languishing in the attic.

My aim, then, was to relate to film personalities who warmed up to the idea of a short story, and were game to narrate their stories or write one themselves. A majority of the stories here have been narrated to me in detail, which I was permitted to expand and use the occasional pinch of dramatic licence. All of them have been edited in a manner so there is stylistic coherence. Unlike the admonishment of the lady with the Chihuahua, there has been no invasion of my thoughts, ideas, or language.

Inevitably, there will be the accusation, 'You must have written them all yourself. Film people can't narrate stories from their lives...' Sorry to break the bubble, they do, once that essential degree of intimacy and trust have been struck. While receiving the crucial final touches to the stories by wonder editor Dipa Chaudhuri, I could well have accused her, 'But your punctuations are so much yours, not mine or anyone else's.' That would have been a silly thing to do. Editing is a fine, but fast-diminishing art. The stories went through a structural process, albeit remaining allied to the narrator's personality.

Through the couple of years which went into *Faction*, my constant question to myself was: Are stories narrated by others as satisfying as writing your own collection? To be honest, the answer is no and yes. No, because you're on a leash, and are vulnerable to making errors. One of the film personalities was rattled on reading the draft I had made, 'It's beautiful,' he said over a trans-Atlantic phone-line, 'You've added your imagination to it...' So why was he sounding upset? Turned out that although what he had said while narrating the story sounded harmless, in print it would appear awful. Understandably, he wanted a few lines cut which could possibly hurt someone in real life. Done. Another requested the deletion of an intemperate line uttered by her, in jest, during her narration. But it sounded below-the-belt in print. Done, corrected. 'Thanks,' came the reply. 'Now, I just have to make sure my mother doesn't read it. I'll have to keep the book hidden.'

Such spokes in the wheel—or no's—weren't an issue. On the more stubbornly purist side, it's just that as a writer, I felt I was feeding on other people's stories, when I have so many—good or bad—to tell myself. After writing *Two Mothers and Other Stories,* I wanted to start on a novel which I have to save from extinction within myself. Stories I must tell before I die, that sort of thing. I try to be dismissive about this, keep warning myself: Don't give yourself or your stories that much importance. The paradox is I know they have to be told, not as a 200-pager exercise in catharsis, but in the firm belief that these are stories about some extraordinary people who led extraordinary lives.

On the 'yes' side, the upper was getting to know the film personalities more closely than I ever could have, the talks, on occasion, making me feel in the exalted position of a therapist, beavering away at moments and entire life spans which they had kept concealed. Not that any of the writers would quite agree with that; they have so much more to say and relate. Hopefully they will some day, and not necessarily in the mode of roseate autobiographies.

Over the decades, on the jagged beat of profiles, interviews and critiques of film personalities, it has been a religion to stick to the word count and the nature of the publication. An interview in a newspaper has to be remarkably different from a monthly magazine's (though it's hard to tell the difference nowadays). Interviews on the phone and mail, like it or not, have lowered standards. Once, a news editor would see through that in a paper, a magazine editor would spike a shallow interview and deny the writer his yearly increment. No such führers now. More's the pity. Neither were copies scanned by the PRs, or scores of interviews organised on the eve of a film's opening week.

If I bring that up, it's merely to make the point that the interview style would not have worked for *Faction*. There were no questions—sharp or blunt—and there were no answers—evasive or sensational.

The meetings for the stories followed a route—so tell me a story from your life, or from another's. Initially, this was met with bafflement—what kind of story exactly? Exactly the point—anything which the narrator believes is worth telling. One narrated a story, but vacillated after it was written. 'Too personal,' perhaps, but eventually said, 'So what! It stays. It's important to me.' That was gratifying in a business ridden with image-preservation.

One more upper was the permission granted by Bharati Jaffrey, with no qualifications at all, to reconstruct a story which her father, the adorable Ashok Kumar had written in fits and starts, never quite reaching its conclusion. The legendary actor who passed away 12 years ago at the age of 90, relished writing stories, many of which have remained on paper. He enjoyed the company of litterateurs. Saadat Hassan Manto and he collaborated on film projects. What Manto and Dadamoni could have done with a film script adapted from *A Calcutta Story*, tantalises the imagination.

At the end of driving *Faction* to its last words, above all there is a feeling of satisfaction. Or is there? Mick Jagger's line, 'I Can't Get No Satisfaction' interrupts as soon as I say that. Complacency is alien to me, not exactly an ideal state for a writer-editor. That wretched lack of complacency keeps me restless and wanting to do more.

Although a sequel to *Faction* would be feasible, more stories from more film personalities—it would keep me tethered to others' lives. I have enough facts to fictionalise, and enough fiction to make factual. Yet, this is one effort I can look back on with affection.

To share others' lives was rewarding because it enlightened me—that I'm not alone in my spells of emotional turbulence.

An agile re-inventor, he has carromed between death-defying action and life-affirming romance, bunging in comedy as well. Variously known as the *khiladi,* the street smarty and the gallant lover, his best include *Khiladi* (of course), *Dhadkan, Rowdy Rathore* and *Once Upon a Time in Mumbai Dobaara!* Presciently, his short story kicks off the collection, both in terms of inception and delivery on the dot of deadline.

AKSHAY KUMAR

Love on the 7.45 a.m. local

The 7.45 a.m. local train, Andheri-Victoria Terminus, carried its regular passengers. This was on Mumbai's subsidiary Harbour line. At that hour, passengers in the first class compartment wore upright combat-with-the-world postures, registering that another day had begun in a paradise where the threshings to survive aren't an instinct. They're the law—it's live and let die out here.

The train looked the same every morning—unswept, unwashed, un-un. So did the commuters, unsmiling and unaffected by the seasons. The boy, Rajiv Hari Bhatia, recognised most of them, but none spoke to him. The city of perpetual needs doesn't encourage friendship. He kept to himself, observing, but never interfering in the private worlds inhabited by fellow travellers. Newspapers would be read, some would dog-ear a crime story paperback; others like him would gaze at the compartment of expressionless wonders. The 12-year-old boy, uniformed in white-shirt-khaki-trousers-sienna-brown-tie-fading-brass-badge was lanky; he would have travelled by school bus had the contractor agreed to a slight detour, but didn't. 'Too much petrol waste,' he explained. Just as well, the boy liked trains, the writhing snakes connecting a hundred destinations. So many people, he smiled to himself, humming 'Eleanor Rigby', 'Ah, look at all the lonely people... where do they all come from? All the lonely people...where do they all belong?', taught at the piano by the school's music teacher. The boy didn't make it to the choir, but he did hum when no one could hear him.

The train wove in and out of replica stations, ejecting hordes, but also admitting hot-eyed throngs to occupy the green rexine-padded seats. The atmosphere at Mumbai local railway stations is armour-strong, invincible, but trembling at the prospect of yet another morning-evening peak hour pounding of feet, the sport of elbowing, kicking, cursing, a fugitive grope at a woman's breast. By 9 a.m. it would be mayhem on the local trains—Western, Central and Harbour lines—marrying the suburbs to the central city which thrives on mercantile trade. Mumbai is described as the commercial capital of India. Without the trains carrying office-goers to their employment desks, the metropolis would come to a standstill. If there is a railway strike or a derailment, finished! Life's paralysed. Once the strike is over, or the derailment damage cleared, newspaper headlines crow with relief. The city is now limping back to normal. But hasn't it always been on crutches?

This was back in the 1960s. Five decades later, the suburb-city connect is even more acutely dependent on its trains, despite plots and plans to create alternate trade hubs in Navi Mumbai and the Bandra-Kurla complex. Mumbai doesn't change except for its name. Its development is asphalt and haphazard, not catered towards a citizen's convenience. Bribing contractors, a corrupt municipal bureaucracy, are a legacy of the British Raj. In this scheme of things, nothing can beat the good old local trains, which have not been adequately upgraded. They are functional, they are a constant. Commuters increase every minute, services don't.

Rajiv would hop into the train at Andheri, alighting at King's Circle station to make his way to Don Bosco School. He carried a khaki canvas satchel obese with books which were invariably festooned with red correction marks and remarks that he should 'pull up his socks' in every subject but English composition for some odd reason. Reading and writing came as naturally as breathing to him, befuddling him: how come something so facile paid that stray rich dividend in the school report cards? Strange. Like that socks stuff. Sure, he'd pull them up, but only after they were darned.

Once inside the 7.45 a.m. local, Rajiv would see a young woman about twenty or so...she was pleasant: simple, petite, no cosmetic cloak over her valentine face. She would be attired through the working-day week in three different floral printed *salwar kameezes*—tulips, rosebuds and micro daffodils. Her polycotton *dupattas* would be crumpled, just like her mouth once in a while when she looked into a book and presumably found the words disturbing. She would take off her tortoise-shell spectacles once, at times twice, to pat her eyes with a handkerchief, more out of habit than need. She could have done with some refrigerated rose water. Cooling.

Rajiv could not make out what she read because the slim books were always covered with brown paper. These were perhaps romantic novels, a very popular read those days, lent out by circulating libraries full of tall dark men about to plant their lips on a trembling beauty in a hip-accentuating gown, all spin-offs of Clark Gable puckering up for Vivien Leigh in *Gone With The Wind*. Although the slim paperbacks were covered with brown paper, they didn't have a long life since they passed from one new hand to another everyday. The binding rebelled out of sheer overuse.

The books must have been Mills & Boons. Meanwhile, a snow-haired man at the other end of the compartment devoured Gulshan Nanda stories in Hindi about a hero, heroine, villain and cataclysmic circumstances. This was a mobile library, many of the readers turning pages of newspapers, attempting to solve crosswords, and often nudging companions into clichéd conversations on politics *du jour*. 'This Indira Gandhi, nice lady, but too *kadak, yaar*. But *kya karen*, there is no alternative. TINA factor, ha ha! Congress *apna mai baap*,' would be the majority opinion, a dissenting voice proclaiming, '*Dekho*, Jayaprakash Narayan is a good man. He will bring about change. Nehru *parivar ka raj kab tak chalega?*' Rajiv noticed that there was a singular lack of warmth, friendship...and romance in the train—in his mind an ideal location for love stories to bloom. He wished the young woman in the floral clothes would fall in love, she had to...but how? When? Hurry up, O Tulip Kumari, the boy longed for her to look happy. No one at home seemed to be except on occasion his parents, when his father brought home his Diwali bonus, and gold ear-rings for the boy's mother. Love—what is it? What is it? Rajiv had to find out before he could set out to look for it; he needed a reference point.

The girl, the girl-woman...remained stubbornly friendless. At times, the Don Bosco boy imagined that she nodded at him; he did not respond. What if she didn't smile back at him? Rejection? No thanks. He named her Latika. Naah, not suitable. Neena, too ordinary. Priya, are you crazy? Those movie heroines are called Priya or Pinky. Anamika? Hell, that's a movie's name. Tulip Kumari? Rude rude, rude. Let her be... 'let it be, let it be', humming Lennon-McCartney...let it be.

The boy was in seventh standard. Like half his class, he preferred to spend time in the school's compound, playing volley ball and tennis ball cricket. Increasingly, the satchel was becoming an enemy. He could throw it away on the railway tracks when the train carried him to and fro from school. No point, it would bounce back. Seventh standard meant subjects he could not figure: mathematics, geography, history, chemistry, physics...what an overdose of education. Geometry, he detested. He did not care if he could not tell the difference between theorems, and would be pulled up. Better to pull up the socks. But how? He scowled to himself, it's all so dull-dull-dull. Look...just look at that girl...that woman today in that same old rosebud *salwar kameez*. She just keeps reading. Lady, let's exchange our lives. He would read, she could logarithm.

Then it was June, July maybe. Rajiv doesn't remember the exact date or month, but he can recall that it was raining as if the heavens had opened up to shed tears. He was in his blue plastic raincoat, serving him since the last three years. The young woman had a white, blue and pink umbrella next to her. As always, she got off at Bandra station that day, but forgot her umbrella. Before she could disembark, another regular passenger—a man about twenty-five—leapt to pick up the umbrella. He placed his hand on her shoulder and before she could be affronted, he said, 'Excuse me, you have forgotten something…I don't want you to get wet.' She broke into the sunniest smile on the cloudy day and said, 'Thank you.' The man returned to his seat, chuffed as if he had saved her life.

The boy had seen him before, but his gaze had never stopped on him—just another white-collar worker. Clerk, secretarial assistant, accountant, shit—who the hell cares. But today the dormouse was special, gallant; he went up notches in the boy's esteem. The chivalrous one back at his window seat, he was the hero of the day. Others looked at him accusingly, as if he had stripped in public, but after that split-second-long blink of reprimand, returned to their newspapers, prayer beads, or just looked anxious about what the pouring rain would do to them when they alighted. No taxis, no buses, difficult, difficult, but then such is life, such is resilience. The gallant one was stocky, distinctively adult and serious, something the boy couldn't be at this point. The man folded and refolded his newspaper. He wasn't reading, he was probably rushing a thousand times over to touch the girl on her shoulder. The umbrella had played the part of Cupid. A violin concerto could be heard above the train's clat-clatter.

The young woman, Rajiv was sure, reached wherever she had to, safe and dry. The drying daffodils on her *kurta* watered, she must be smiling,thrilled inwardly that someone had talked to her bossily, '*I don't want* you to get wet.' He must have been the first man in her life, she the first girl in his. Such incipient encounters don't have back stories. If there are any, they have to be rescinded. Romances are perfect when there's a connection at first sight, the past erased faster than the boy's arithmetic errors. He would only marry for love some day, someone out there was made for him, he'd find her when he came of age though it was taking an eternity, and that too in slow-motion. Really who knows? There could be another girl with an umbrella on this train, on the railway platform, on the traffic junction he crossed to reach school. The boy would know she's the one as soon as he saw her. He'd bend down on his knees, promise to buy her the moon and stars. And she would say, 'I don't need the moon and stars. You're good enough.' They would fall insanely in love, they would be hopelessly devoted to each other till their dying day. In a gingerbread home, two obedient kids and cars, domestic aides and cats and dogs would bow-meow through a manicured garden—with real tulips. She would darn his socks when he was sixty-four.

As the train braked, screaming to let another fast local thunder past, the boy came back to earth, his thought bubble going, 'No harm in dreaming, is there?'

Next day, the rain persisted. She occupied the same seat, so did the dormouse hero, both looking away at nothing in particular. No smiles, nods or stolen glances. Just calculated indifference. Hang on, hang on, what's going on? When she alighted at Bandra, so did he, presumably gambling half-a-day's salary-cut at the office. Sweet, so sweet, Rajiv could taste the sugar.

The following day, the two were sitting next to each other. They talked haltingly, the boy conjectured, about the weather, their jobs and families. Their hobbies? No, no, hobbies are bunkum, blah-blah. Music, reading, sports, nothing out of line...they couldn't possibly ever go trekking, too hazardous. The local trains, given to unprecedented delays and derailments, were adventurous enough.

The man and girl-woman alighted again at Bandra. They must have chatted over filter coffee at the Udupi restaurant just facing the station; they must have held hands; they might have even kissed on the rocks at the Bandra Bandstand seafront, where lovers nestle, ignoring the savage sun.

Next month, in the compartment, their bodies touched. When he thought no one was looking, the man cradled her palm in his. Rajiv pretended not to notice, but was startled when, one morning, the man wrapped his arm tightly around her hips. She seemed grateful about his bravado, shifted closer to him. Their bodies seemed soldered, in heat. Oddly, the boy wasn't envious, he was privy to a love ride which would reach its destination. It had to. The train snaked on, hissing its metallic beat. Undoubtedly, on maturing, the boy would caress his own girl in tulips. She would sit by him, chattering away shyly, bodies in contact, on the 7.45 a.m. local.

The boy wasn't surprised by the peregrinations of love. She carried the umbrella even though it was desert dry, to protect herself ostensibly from the Bandra Bandstand sun. When she alighted from the train, the man would pick up the white, pink and blue umbrella and press it open for her with a manly flourish. This ritual continued—till without so much as a by-your-leave, the man and the young woman vanished for a month and some more. Rajiv missed their febrile foreplay. Then he forgot them. He had to, intermittently hoping that the man did right by the woman in tulips. He would kill the bastard if he had dropped her, if he had caused any form of harm to her, if he had taken advantage of her, if he had left her crying. Where was she? Please, please lord, he prayed, he wanted to see the girl once again. He had to know if she was unscarred...alive.

Then they re-entered the train, behaving intimately as if the compartment was the ante-chamber to their honeymoon suite. She had changed into a flaming red *zari*-encrusted polyester sari and a tight paisley printed *choli*. She wore gold jewellery. No more spectacles, perhaps her parents had bought her contact lenses in dowry. The man held her hands with authority; his hand would move to her bare back. Her hand didn't leave his thigh. It didn't take a genius' IQ to deduce that theirs was a serial honeymoon...it hadn't ended. No one could object to their cooing and clasping. See, see those thin gold bands on their fingers and the *sindoor* in her *maang*. They looked mad for each other. To share their formal union, they had even passed a box of saffron *pedhas* to their fellow travellers. By the time the box reached Rajiv, it was empty. Upset, she said, 'I'll get a box just for you,' but never kept that promise. No worries, those *pedhas* looked fungused, the boy consoled himself.

After a fortnight, she moved from red polyester to crisp cotton, faintly embroidered saris. He was still in his white shirts, dark pleated trousers and still carried a battered leather briefcase: a working-class couple, soaked in love, going their separate ways for the office hours.

At this juncture, Rajiv was in the ninth standard. One morning, the couple seemed to be more genial than usual. The man asked, with avuncular concern, 'How is school? All well?' The boy nodded evasively. What else could he do? If he had said he was sick of school, would they have cared? 'Hello, young man,' the woman smiled at him fondly. 'Do you like trains?' Rajiv shrugged non-committally, hoping that they had not sensed his abiding interest in their girl-meets-Mr Perfect-to-live-wonderfully-ever-after bagatelle.

Two more years elapsed, the boy was about to complete his school studies. His socks had been pulled up to his knees now. If theorems had to be understood, so be it. The Don Boscoite would pore into his textbooks during the morning commute. By now he was just about mildly interested in his exemplary couple, role models for his future. *Na, na,* think exams right now, pass with flying colours. Colours? Do they fly? Quit carping, boy. In any case, how about becoming a man first? Love or arranged marriage, whatever, he'd marry some day, he'd find a woman, he'd find warmth—he looked forward to clothed sexual intimacy on the Bandra Bandstand rocks. Home, too small, too crowded. Even with his wife, there would be that *chukker* of stolen kisses, stolen fondling. Hey, now shut up. You a pervert or what?

Helplessly, Rajiv eavesdropped on his couple's conversations. He couldn't move to another story or turn stone deaf, could he? She had issues with her in-laws, she argued for a separate home, privacy, independence…she wished to become a mother, but not before they had a home of their own. He'd grouse that their salaries, put together, would push them further into the suburbs. There would be draconian home-loan bank interests. He suggested that they be patient till his next promotion and increment...which never came. They'd buzz on about the obstacles. Enough is enough. Who needs to hear such pap? Enough is enough. He'd play music on his Discman, the couple silenced by Kurt Cobain's guitar blasts.

And then it rained furiously. Rajiv's raincoat had changed to a casual wind cheater. The couple bounded into the compartment to their rexine seats. The woman's umbrella was white Dacron printed with sprays of roses. The man-and-woman exchanged perfunctory remarks with other commuters about the merciless weather. She picked up the umbrella and tiffin carrier when she alighted at Bandra station. She nodded at her man with the briefcase; he nodded robotically, and returned to solving a crossword puzzle. Next he lit a cigarette, dragged on it deeply. He wore a new florid tie. His briefcase was faux alligator-skin and he jabbed away at a calculator as if the nation's finances depended on his multiplications.

Rajiv wanted to ask the man if he was okay, if he had come to terms with domestic differences, but didn't. None of his damn business. If the man had replied with, 'Excuse me?' the boy would have either perished on the spot or punched him hard, very hard on the jaw. Desist kid, don't poke your bulbous nose into their lives, not right, not done. Romance comes with an expiry date. So what's the big deal? Everyone has problems —minor or major. The boy had his...how to keep his father, an accountant with UNICEF, optimistic. A father who would have been so, so proud when the boy moved on to college, and did the right thing. IIT, IIM, IAS, so many IIIs.

Quit caring—for even an errant minute—about how this man wearing a stupid tie is now treating his woman in a crisp sari...and just a speck of *sindoor*? For everyone, everything works out. They have to be each other's support systems. In any case, the two can't possibly continue to be like a couple in that first flush of love. Somewhere deep within, they do care for each other, love each other. A love story the schoolboy had witnessed so closely couldn't fade; the differences would be resolved. They always are. Perhaps...now now, don't worry about them, worry about yourself.

The next day, it rained mercilessly over the 7.45 a.m. Andheri-Victoria Terminus again. The woman forgot to pick up her umbrella when she alighted at Bandra station. The man noticed that, but did not move at all. He lit a cigarette, saw her leave in the rain without any protection, and looked away.

Before the man alighted at King's Circle station, he cast a look at the umbrella, almost picked it up, but didn't.

A white nylon umbrella with red rose buds lay abandoned on the green rexine seat. The Don Bosco student picked it up. Why let it go to the lost-and-found department? No one goes there. He took it away with him, shoving it into his khaki satchel. He would keep the umbrella. The man would never unfurl it for the woman with a flourish. The man would never say to her, 'I don't want you to get wet in the rain.' If she did, fell ill, and died, so be it. Why should he rush to her protection? No one's Mr Perfect.

Then, like a July cloud, the boy wept. A love story had ended.

Endowed with Adonis looks and a flair for controlled, implosive performances, the nation's most-loved super model moved to movie acting, grappled with it initially but now wears the suit of a sensitive actor perfectly. Arguably his best are *Rock On!* and *Rajneeti*.

ARJUN RAMPAL

New York days, New York nights

ARRIVAL. The immigration clearance officer is looking him up and down. Redder than a basket of strawberries, he's scanning Apurva Raj Singh sternly. Apurva's unfazed. He's been through this so many times before. Just another acupressure of overseas travel. The man behind the counter doesn't like what he sees. They never do, part of the clearance deck code. The inquiring gaze has to be pure steel—it's suggesting go back east young man, you're getting negative evaluation here.

Then to Apurva's relief, and to that of scores of jet-lagged souls in the python queue, the stamp comes down on the passport. *Thashaak*. The officer even says, 'Have a good stay.' Yeah sure, buddy.

He shouldn't resent the officer; he's just doing his job. The immigrant—not yet but maybe, agenda on hold right now—also has to acknowledge that he's not exactly presentable. All of 25, he has kicked up jobs back home, hasn't shaved, or organised his hair—should've done that on the flight, should've requested a complimentary comb—his pair of jeans are scruffy and his fire-engine-red T-shirt could do with a rapid rinse. Never mind, others in the queue aren't in tuxedoes either. He's fine, he's aspiring to conquer the world. 'It's up to you, New York, New York...' The strawberry officer flashes a polite smile. 'Thank you...sir,' Apurva expresses his gratitude, collects a single suitcase from the conveyor belt, walks past the customs breezily—not that he has a single item to declare—ambles towards the automatic doors which part like an estranged couple. And he's breathing made-in-America air.

Here's the land of limitless opportunities. 'My little town blues; they're melting away,' his inner voice sings off-key, like the ditty 'New York, New York'...they liked it so much, they named it twice.

Apurva's clued in. He knows where he is, and is conditioned already. Now for a big juicy bite of the Big Apple. There have been quickie trips before, at first touristy, then walk-the-fashion-ramp assignments. Today, he casts a sour-grapes look at the cabs. Not too many dollars to spare. Save every cent. The bus bound for Manhattan will be his first solo survey of NYC, no one to share his 'Wow' or 'Man, it's mind-blowing.' 'New York, New York'...they liked it so much...awww shut up. Get serious. About time to get your life on course. Quit the 'wow wows.'

It's 7 a.m. The outskirts are as sleepy as the Mumbai suburbs. Mornings are the same everywhere. Stretches of squalor remain where they were. No city clean-ups, redevelopment, or what? Ghettos zip by—row houses, half-burnt, half-crumbling. Traffic clogs on the highway permit Apurva to photograph the renewed impressions in his memory. What a disconcerting start; it has to improve. And it does the moment New York's famed skyscraper-lined horizon comes into sight—grey, super-tall, gorgeous. He's bound for Manhattan. Not Brooklyn, Bronx, Queens, New Jersey or Staten Island. It's the prime borough for Apurva Raj Singh. 'Just call me Apu,' he'll tell the New Yorkers.

The bus is half empty. Or half full. He's brimming with hope: 'I want to wake up in a city that doesn't sleep. It's buzzy, throbbing. My day will come. I'll be king of the hill. Top of the heap...' Hang on, he's dehydrated. Anxiety does that to him. The weather's no ally. Cold-cold-cold, spring is giving way to autumn. And that drizzle, the drops zigzagging artily on the glass panes. He clings on to optimism, 'Hey, it's me guys! Start spreading the news...'

The bus slows down. It's entering a tunnel. Darkness discomforts and comforts. A small-town gawky, skinny boy from Deolali, from an exceptionally good-looking family with Dutch antecedents, would once run behind trains, attempting to stop them. Reason? Run away? Perhaps, but the sound of wheels bearing heavily down on metal rails would drown his helpless pleas. He'd cry easily then. Not any more. An aunt had berated him, 'Don't display your emotions. Or else they'll call you a sissy.'

During school vacations, while playing imaginary games in the Deolali hills—riding dozing donkeys, believing he was the Wild West's Lone Ranger, swimming, cycling, moped zooms through a wilderness which became his private playground—

Apurva would convince himself, 'I'm strong, strong, strong... no one dare call me a sissy.' Summer and winter, the heat and the cold were endemic. No worries about getting burnt or being deep-frozen. Then on reaching seventh standard, he experienced his first crush: his teacher Poonam, peach-complexioned, Goldilocks hair and light eyes. Heaven was on his mind but crushes don't last. Poonam married a non-entity and that girl with the fluorescent smile in the neighbourhood didn't even look his way. Just whizzed past like those heartless trains.

Eventually, Apurva left Deolali. His parents had agreed to go their separate ways. As simple as that. So his sister left with their father for Delhi. His mother, an English language teacher, selected the Kodaikanal International School for him, away from his private Wild West. To his surprise, he cleared his examinations with distinction. Mother wasn't surprised though; she wasn't a worrier at all. Had her son longed for the moon and stars, she would've bought them for him at a discounted rate.

School done, Apurva enrolled in Delhi's Hindu College and its hostel. When he was ragged by his seniors, his instinct was to sprint back to the Deolali hills. Delhi wasn't for him but he couldn't disappoint his mother. The son hung on, toughened. Soon the mirror reflected another image. He didn't turn his face away from what he saw. Then one day he caught the eye of a fashion guru at a local discotheque. Apurva was invited to model for the cover of a city magazine. In return, he would get to keep the clothes worn for the shoot, the kind which accentuated his looks. Yesterday's gawky boy had arrived.

He was even called 'drop-dead gorgeous', ha ha, signing his first autograph at Delhi's airport.

Apurva of chiselled jaw, olive skin and ramrod frame modelled on the ramp and for print ads. He was knighted India's Face of 1994. He taught his mentor tennis, and the two were seen at the right places at the right time. Two men together? Must be gay. Speculations intensified. So be it.

Next stop: Mumbai with no room to spare. Apurva stayed at a friend's house on Marine Drive for four days, then cast anchor at the Lokhandwala complex in the suburbs. He was happening. Pardoxically, he wasn't. An intense relationship with a woman who doted on him, ended. There was no bitterness but he wasn't the same anymore. He felt the need to wrestle with his ego as well as his fears.

He travelled to Dharamsala. It wasn't the sanctuary he had longed for. He felt he was drowning deep. He wanted answers. He soul-searched. He listened, impatiently though, to advice from strangers who believed they had unlocked the mysteries of existence. He noted some of their suggestions, even shards of poems and proverbs in a notebook. But did he ever turn to it for advice? Heck, who needs advice? Forget it. Desire is the root of all trouble. Accept that. Introspect. He asked himself the eternal questions, 'Who am I?', 'What am I?' He felt he was in contact with his spiritual side. Buddy, that still doesn't guarantee simple answers, or instant solutions. There's no shortcut to nirvana.

Back to modelling, back to flutes of bubbly and idle chatter. Apurva wanted out. A face decomposes fast in Mumbai's insular world of fashion and modelling. Fortuitously, he was selected by a top-line international modelling agency; they would make him a face in Eurasia. Over to London. No dice. Six months and hundreds of auditions later, he couldn't afford the rent of his Notting Hill apartment. Apurva hit rock bottom. That's when he knew where to head. He boarded a flight at Heathrow for JFK Airport. 'I am leaving today. I want to be part of the buzz.'

This has to be it. *The* final touchdown. *The* destination. He pretends to be confident but is aware that he isn't. He blinks rapidly, shielding his eyes from the bright sun as the bus emerges from the tunnel. 'New York, New York'...they liked it so much...awww shut up. Say something else. How about, 'Let there be light?'

Or, 'A doorbell of my own. A loft, hope, and no one beside me.' He finds a transient home; soon he'll buy a loft of his own. Meanwhile, he grapples with the residues of that heartbreak. Relationships, relationships, they either lead to marriage or a void. 'Do not disturb me,' he wishes, but badly wants to be disturbed. The phone is obstinately silent for days, weeks, months. No calls for work at all. One of those don't-call-us-we'll-call-you situations. He goes through the *déjà* experienced. Or so it seems. What to do? No dollars, no smiles. Survival of sorts is possible by hanging out at the nearby film school, the legendary NYU. Occasionally, he doctors scripts, fetching him $20 to $30 an assignment.

India's Face of 1994 hangs on. He's a loser. He insults himself, then consoles himself, 'Don't be so hard on yourself. If there's a god above this Manhattan skyline, he'll give you a sign.' God does. Moseying around Amsterdam Square, he sees a statue coated with pigeon shit. Could that be a sign? Must be: some days you're the pigeon, some days the statue. Fine, and so the conclusions: care a shit about what's happening (difficult), do something spectacular before returning home (very difficult) or just die here (way to croak!).

At the NYU campus, he hears of a job which has to be firmed the next day. Apurva is safe for a while. A dog-sitter he shall be at the Soho apartment of an Argentinean couple taking off to Buenos Aires for a month. The pay is piffling but the refrigerator is stocked with food and drinks which could last through a scorching summer. Moreover, he doesn't have to pay rent for his boxy apartment which he can now vacate with pleasure.

The dog Mylo is a pariah, a long-haired Dachshund, morose and indifferent to his guardian. Not for long. Apurva teaches him a trick: how to sit stationary on his shoulder. For three weeks, the dog and his sitter watch TV, thrill to James Bond flicks on video cassette, pig out on steaks and guzzle beer. Mylo is ruined. He becomes an alcoholic, barking violently, and chewing the furniture if he is denied his pre-lunch lager. As it happens, the Argentinean couple return a week earlier than the month they had committed, scream at Apurva, refuse to pay the salary promised and threaten to report him to the police but know no legal charge can be levelled. It would be ridiculous to tell any court that a dog-sitter has made a moral mess of a Dachshund. 'Get the hell out, you you...,' they don't know whether to call him 'rotten Indian', so settle on 'arsehole'. Mylo goes into a sulk. Beer binges over.

Apurva is heartbroken when he leaves the apartment with his toothbrush, deodorant, a carry bag of three or four changes of clothes, and the coolest attitude this side of the emptied refrigerator. Mylo snarls, barks, whines, whimpers on his bartender's departure, and will probably chew the furniture to cope with his withdrawal symptoms.

Now this is a tough one. Nowhere to go. Except Central Park.

Eight, maybe ten months gone. It's April. Time and Apurva's life stand still. New York summers can be harsh but the weather doesn't bother him. He checks into Central Park, no credit cards required. He knows it is as much a jogging track for the elite as it is a refuge for tramps, and a hunting ground for criminals out to mug anyone who looks vulnerable or unarmed. Nevertheless, the park founded in 1857—the year of the Indian Mutiny, how did they know?—sprawling over an astonishing green belt of 850 acres is the city's pride, freckled with walking and bicycling tracks, lakes, ponds, woods, theatre, food halts...a veritable cut-out from a fairy tale book. Tough cops brandishing tougher batons patrol the park. Yet the rising crime rate isn't reassuring. No cop around, though, when he enters. Just as well...he would deal with the wait-and-watch, as and when.

Movies have been shot in and around Central Park. Isn't this the spot where Orson Welles rescued Rita Hayworth from a posse of goons? The film? *The Lady from Shanghai*, was it? His mother's favourite. *When Harry Met Sally* was located here too. His sister loved it. Oh, so many movies...forget them...

their scripts are all figments of glossy imagination. Right now, he remembers his aunt's warning, 'Don't display your feelings…' He'll stay in the park as long as it's humanly possible. He has to be careful, avoid all eye contact. Banish the thought of striking up a conversation, dude. Neither would he smile nor grimace. He'd just *be*. No one would bother him. That's the law of the jungle, isn't it?—don't mess with anyone and no one will mess with you. Oh really?

The afternoon segues into evening, then night. Apurva doesn't budge from the bench he has selected close to one of the several exit points. He isn't thirsty or hungry, can't afford to be. Just $15 to go. He has to save them up for the next day. Anything could happen. He could be arrested, thrown into jail. Perhaps the Indian Embassy would be informed and they'd organise his ticket back home. Perhaps he'd finally hear from one of those agents. How? Somehow! Or perhaps Mylo would embark on a quest for his bartender. What doesn't kill you makes you stronger. That's that. Surprisingly, he sinks into sleep…surprising because whenever he is more tired than usual, he can't sleep at all.

Apurva wakes up at 7 a.m. He feels invigorated. He has slept like a newborn. He likes this plein-air cradle. He could spend the rest of his life here, sprout a beard, occupy the bench, and gape at the world passing him by. Those peroxide blondes in shorts are already running past him. He is invisible.

Five dollars buy him breakfast and another five, a phone call to his sister in Delhi. He needs a ticket back home, his visa is fast expiring. He doesn't tell her he's on the streets.

It's a Sunday. She can't gather the ticket money right away. Maybe tomorrow. He would have to check with the airline office.

Apurva's close to tears but guffaws instead over the phone, 'It's been a blast here and now I'm homesick.'

His sister pauses, then says crisply, 'Don't lie. You're in trouble.'

He counters, 'No trouble at all.'

'Are you sure?'

'Yes...why?'

'Swear on me.'

'I swear on you,' he lies.

'I'll try my best to get the ticketing done...but I can't promise.'

'Try.'

'Are you in trouble?'

'Yes. I'm fucking stranded here.'

'I'll get the ticketing done.'

Another day, another night then at Central Park. And that should be the end of the New York dream. 'These vagabond shoes; They are longing to stray; Right through the heart of it; New York, New York...' Not quite the ending he had hoped for but so what? He's no hero; he would've liked to be one. For the time being, Apurva is determined not to buckle under. He is light and easy after a wash in one of the park's restrooms. According to the mirror, India's Face of 1994 looks good. No one is hitting on him though. Neither man nor woman. Just as well. Who needs complications? Relationships, relationships, relationships, no thanks.

A hike through the park, watching kids on the swings and seesaws, he notices that infants in prams don't cry like they do back home. They gurgle angelically or glare imperiously. Mothers look ferociously protective. Perhaps they even carry revolvers to deal with child snatchers. Who knows? Who cares? None of Apurva's business. Avoid those vigilante mommy eyes at this very minute. Back to the bench. It must be a sign from God again: all the benches are taken except his. He watches people but with a gaze so glassy that he could have been looking anywhere, an art he had mastered on those fashion ramps which he had ignited with his presence. No emotions, emotions...that's in the rule book.

Apurva fishes out the long-ignored notebook and a complimentary airline pen from his carry bag. Writing would help pass the afternoon. So many empty pages...only the first two or three are scribbled over with supposed words of wisdom during his brief stay in Dharamsala. He starts to write, 'Here I am...' and stops. With the pen's nib, he scratches covertly on the wooden armrest, 'THIS IS MY BENCH.' For a moment he feels rich and famous. Noon elapses. He wanders over to the water fountain, chewing on a stick of gum which was loitering in the innards of the carry bag, waiting for night to fall. The bench is at a distance from a cluster of tall trees—yet another sign from God, perhaps. 'Thank you boss,' he mumbles. 'If I were near a tree after sunfall, I'd be breathing carbon monoxide. Or that's what they taught me at school. Wrong or right, thanks boss!'

Is he disappointed that no one has asked him to vacate the bench, that no one has noticed him, that no one has spread the word, that it was all so eventless? None of the tramps hiding hooch in brown paper bags offered him a swig. No cop pounced on him to inspect his passport. Such tender mercies, don't speak too soon. Get busy, look busy. He makes an effort to record his feelings of disappointment and relief in the notebook again. He can't; he is at a loss for words. Instead, he scratches away furiously, and deep, on the wooden armrest again, 'THIS IS MY BENCH.' The notebook falls to the ground. He picks it up and is about to close it when he halts at some lines of unsolicited advice offered by a traveller on his way back home from Dharamsala.

The train had been half-empty. Or half-full. Apurva had been looking out at the rolling nightscape when a co-traveller, barely out of his teens, had said, 'You seem restless. Don't be,' adding, 'You know how it is. We complain about not having shoes when others don't have feet.'

Apurva had looked away. 'This guy's a pest...he'll subject me to more stale fundas.'

The stranger wore a pair of Levi's and a white *chikan* kurta. A city slicker who had Zenned out and was intent on making the world a happier place. He continued, 'I can see that you don't want to be bothered...so I will just remember a few lines for you...could be useful some day.'

Apurva couldn't have leapt out of the speeding train. He said, 'Go ahead.'

The stranger smiled, 'It's part of a Chinese poem.'

'I don't understand poems.'

'This one's quite simple.'

'I told you, go ahead...'

'Don't be afraid that the horses' hoofs are sinking...

Don't worry because the cart wheels are stuck in the mud...

Imagine if you were alone here without your walking stick,

...trudging through the snow to look at the mountains!'

The recitation was sing-song.

'You liked it?'

Apurva had nodded curtly.

The stranger didn't speak again. Oddly, Apurva who didn't have a head for poetry remembered the lines. He had jotted them down in the notebook.

As Central Park turns dark, the lines don't strike Apurva as an epiphany. They don't even strike him as especially profound him but they do keep him awake. He can't sleep. He waits for light, splashes water on India's Face of 1994 at the restroom and bins the notebook. He doesn't need words. All he needs is a ticket out of Central Park.

It is there, waiting for him at the airline office.

DEPARTURE. There he is going through immigration clearance again. Whatever for? He is leaving New York, New York...they liked it so much, they named it twice.

To this day, Apurva Raj Singh feels he did make his mark in New York. At Central Park, close to one of its several exit points, at a distance from a cluster of tall trees exuding carbon dioxide at night, there's a bench. On its wooden armrest is a legend: 'THIS IS MY BENCH.'

1911–2001

The big daddy of the Bombay movies, his career straddled over six decades, as a matinee idol and as a character actor who defined effortless performances, shifting gears then towards TV serials. Dadamoni's body of work is immense. His best is beyond categorisation. Suffice it to say his collaborations with directors Bimal Roy, Kamal Amrohi, Hrishikesh Mukherjee, BR Chopra, Basu Chatterji, are incomparable.

ASHOK KUMAR

A Calcutta story

When the British quit India, Shubhang Bhowmick did not rejoice. He was forty or a little more and did not read the newspapers or even possess a radio set. He felt no need to keep in touch with an evolving India. Governance changed, but he was certain it would be for the worse. Cynicism? Pessimism? No isms please. He didn't care about them.

The British had done him no harm specifically. The entire world had been unjust to him. No one liked him, least of all himself. In the mornings, he did not look at the mirror, his face sprouting fresh wrinkles, his sagging neck reminding him of a goose, and he could count the strands of his hair. Why remind himself of mortality, every day? Everyone has to die some day. Anyway, the mirror was covered with stains left by neglect and age.

He chose to trim his bushy beard and bushier eyebrows with his mother's steadily rusting scissors. She had died of an unexplained fever ten years ago. His father had died of indigestion exactly ten years before her. They had timed themselves, exactly a decade after each other, and that too on the same calendar date, January 15, 1927 and 1937. Their Independence Day.

On January 15, 1947, the nation was unshackled from the bondage of the colonialists. The East India Company maintained an office in Calcutta. Fleetingly, Shubhang thought about an empty cavernous office space, or perhaps a few lingering *goras* would still be working. Handing over of power and accounts takes time. Meanwhile, the sizeable Anglo-Indian population would continue to colour the city, the women the shade of pale chrysanthemum.

Shubhang wasn't capable of falling in love. He was much too uptight and emotionally cramped. For his physical needs, he would bed Annie Robertson every Sunday in her two-room house a couple of alleys away from Park Street. On other days, she entertained clients more generous than him. Shubhang, her middle-aged regular, never left more than ₹25 when he crept out of the apartment at a time when he could still catch the last tram back home. Annie would laugh, 'Miss the tram, and you sleep on the streets.'

She was two decades younger than him, a cheerful soul who would imitate the Hollywood stars of the era. Her brownish hair she would tease into curls tumbling on her forehead. Her lips she would lipstick into a valentine, and her grey eyes would sparkle without the help of heighteners. A Max Factor crème base hid the scratches and moles on her face. Her tall frame would be draped in a taffeta skirt, topped by a sleeveless shirt with a plunging neckline.

Out in public, the shirt would be covered with a light cashmere sweater, even at the height of summer. She spoke English with a crisp, toasted accent verging on the Cockney. Her father was an Irishman, her alcoholic mother would constantly be in a gin and soda haze. Whenever Annie bickered with righteous indignation, 'But where is my father? He couldn't have abandoned you just like that,' the mother would guffaw, 'Dear Annie, you know how men are. They want pleasure without bearing the pain of responsibility.'

Shubhang was in awe of Annie's outgoing spirit, but played a power game with her. He never complimented her and would never leave an extra rupee on the bedside table. No birthday presents, no Christmas endearments. They had been together for two years, but he would not give her an increment. No problem. She'd nuzzle him, saying, 'If I didn't like that dirty beard of yours, I would have kicked you out long back. Do you know something, my *bhalo* Shoobhong? You're worse than Silas Marner.' She knew of the archetypal tightwad from the George Eliot book she had picked up from the pavement bazaar. She could never complete it, too dense and too sad. As for Shubang, he didn't know who or what she was babbling about. Must be some silly Irishman her father knew. Or it could be her boss at the florist's where she worked during the day, an establishment which thrived on supplying fresh seasonal flowers to the grand old hotels. The British elite was leaving, the hotels would lose business, the flowers would wilt, her boss thought, but she was an optimist, whooping, 'Brown or white. Whatever the complexion of the guests, flowers are a must.'

Shubhang wasn't much of a conversationalist. She was a jabbering machine. He allowed her to rattle on during their bouts of love-making—his ears had inbuilt sound-proof walls. One Sunday, she had yammered on, 'My adorable paramour. How about changing your shirt at least? I can tolerate your black pair of trousers, they hide the dirt, but your shirt is so sooty and stinky.'

He owned three shirts, all in Egyptian white cotton with black stripes, and clumpy leather shoes, the favoured apparel of account clerks. His job at a shipping company wasn't under threat following India's independence. The company belonged to three brothers from a mercantile family with business interests in Calcutta, Bombay and Madras. The Harchandrais had inherited Shubhang Bhowmick from their father who had a sharp eye for employing malleable accountants, a must for traders fudging annual expenditures to save on taxes.

The obsequious clerk had risen gradually to the post of head accountant, with his own little partitioned cabin in the mouldering office. His monthly salary was a handsome ₹400 after tax cuts, of which he would barely spend ₹100. His meals were spartan, the room he lived in at Uttarpara was a hovel and no one knew what he did with his savings. 'Are you hiding all your riches under your bed at home or what?' Annie had boomed. On receiving a churlish glare, she had tickled his beard, 'Oh my hairy-beary one, what will you do with your lolly when you're dead and cremated?'

Methodically, Shubhang had been investing his savings in gold, shares and debentures—that too successfully. He had a fortune amassed in his wooden closet, which he had padlocked. In any case, what could any burglar do with the shares and debentures? The gold he kept in a bank. He ate little, indulging in fried *hilsa* only on Sunday lunch before leaving for Annie's. 'Something's fishy,' she would titter before accepting his first jab of a kiss, and then exult, 'You are a very strange man, but I like you the way you are, ducky. Maybe I'm crazy. Don't you think so, my sweetheart?'

'No, I don't,' he would grunt.

'Well, my friend Carol thinks you are.'

'Carol who?'

'She works with me at the shop. Nice girl, she's my confidante.'

'Good.'

Shubhang-Annie's trysts followed a schedule. She would serve him tea and sponge cake when he arrived unfailingly at 4 p.m. They would make love, and after a recess, once again. On her record player, she would play a Bing Crosby, Nat King Cole or Glenn Miller platter, which he would not hear. If she liked those voices smarming away, so be it as long as she fell into his arms with the same weekly passion.

Turmoil of the political kind throughout the country did not affect their evenings. The only sign of restlessness was expressed by Annie, she was contemplating migrating to Great Britain. 'I'm tired of life here,' she announced one Sunday over tea. 'No future here. Carol's uncle is in Manchester. He might find something for us to do there.'

'But what about me?' Shubhang blurted out without thinking.

'What about me?' she imitated his self-righteous tenor. 'You don't think beyond your fat nose, do you? All I am for you is a Sunday pastime. When I said 'us', I meant you and I. Carol's happy with her boyfriend here.'

Shubhang did not reply. This conversation would have led to their first argument. A conflict, he couldn't handle. But he had to say no loud and clear when she came up with a plan, 'Come with me Shoobhong. You'll find a much better job there. I'll even pay for your ticket by steamer. I don't want your damn wealth. I want us to be together. I love...'

'I don't,' Shubhang cut her short. 'I'm just one of your customers.'

'Oh I see. If that's the way you see it, the subject is closed.'

They went through the mechanics of love-making, he left. Shubhang erased the Manchester offer from his mind as soon as he was on the tram. Absurd. Why should he even think of leaving his homeland? What was she thinking about?

Next Sunday, Shubhang crossed Park Street, perfectly in time for his weekly addiction. She would not bring up the Manchester plan, he would not let her. He paid her, didn't he? All accounts clear.

Manchester was not on her mind that evening. The tea ceremony over, Annie did not play one of her Bing Crosby or Pat Boone platters. She had an announcement to make, which he could have never expected. Such twists in the plot happened to others, not to him. As he was about to unbutton her shirt, she said, 'I am pregnant.'

'That is not my problem.'

'What do you mean? Not your problem,' her voice rose uncharacteristically. 'It's your child goddamit.'

Always the pragmatist, Shubhang said, coolly, 'How am I to believe that? It could be any of your lovers during the week.'

Annie turned away, put on her cashmere sweater, walked out of her own house, leaving him unfazed. He left perhaps an hour after her. Let her go, he would not change his life. He would find himself another woman, perhaps not immediately, but money could buy him anything. Instead of ₹25, he would have to pay ₹50 an evening. Not a comforting idea, but the accountant consoled himself that the accounts would work out. He would have to ask for a salary hike, the Harchandrais could not afford to lose him. With the hike, he would buy himself a new shirt and shoes. He would have to impress the new woman in order to perfect his Sunday schedules. And he would not go to Sonagachi, where he would be vulnerable to chisellers, even murderers. He would locate a mistress from the Chinese restaurant on Chowringhee—someone not too fancy, but not too coarse either.

Life returned to its usual rhythm. Shubhang worked at the office accounts diligently. His salary was raised to ₹500. His mistress, Sumitra, visited him at his hovel every Sunday at 4 p.m. and left at 8 p.m., before her husband could raise too many questions.

Sumitra had told her family that she was working overtime at a textile shop, which needed her at peak hours on Sunday. Shubhang congratulated himself—he no longer had to spend tram ticket money on Sunday and Sumitra didn't ever ask for more than ₹20. And whenever he remembered Annie, it wasn't for their moments of pleasure together, but for that announcement of pregnancy.

It must have been noon one Sunday when an unexpected visitor arrived. She was petite and pretty and did not look as if she had rung the wrong doorbell. Shubhang's heart leapt, as it always did, on facing the unpredictable.

'I am Carol D'Costa,' the young woman said. 'May I please come in?'

This could be a trap, Shubhang's paranoia was at work. He left the door open as she entered the airless room and sat on a folding chair.

'Annie worked with me at the florist's.'

Shubang's memory was rejigged. He asked cautiously, 'What can I do for you?'

'Mr Bhowmick, Annie passed away...complications during childbirth. The daughter she gave birth to...survived. It's your daughter. The child is with me, but I cannot keep her much longer, although Annie would have wished it that way. I cannot afford to. Neither do I want to give her away to an orphanage. She is yours, you have to accept her.'

Carol was holding back her tears. Shubang wasn't moved, saying blandly, 'The child's not mine, it could be of any of her customers.'

'What!' Carol was startled. 'What customers?'

'The men she saw during the rest of the week.'

'She saw no one else. Ever since she met you...she didn't have to. Mr Bhowmick, she was in love with you...deeply.'

'She never told me that. Not that it would've mattered.'

'You never understood her...it's too late...but what about the child?'

'How do I know you are speaking the truth? What's the proof?'

Carol had come rehearsed, she would convince Bhowmick to accept the new-born. It was useless. She got up from the chair to leave. 'If that's the way you see it, fine,' she said, and headed for the door.

'Wait!' he stopped her.

'I don't have any sort of proof which could be submitted in a court of law,' Carol said strongly. 'All I can say is that Annie didn't want to lose you by giving the impression that she's just an ordinary woman in love. She said you are so miserly that you would run away from any kind of commitment. It's true...she did take on lovers earlier...she prostituted herself to survive... but after you came into your life, she found a job...and that was it. You were her life. After mass at church, she would rush home. If she had told you all this, you wouldn't have listened... you are stone deaf. If she had said anything about love, you would have left her.'

'Love...'

'Let me finish. For two years and more, she waited for her Sunday evenings. Men flirted with her, offered her the moon, but she brushed them aside. She would tell me, 'Carol, I can't live without my Silas Marner.' She even gave up her plans to migrate to England.'

'She shouldn't have.'

'I'll tell you why she did. Because of your reaction,'But what about me?' She didn't want to leave the one man she loved. It's up to you, sir. I'll leave now, it's my afternoon shift at the shop.

I've left the child with my neighbours. We haven't named her yet…that right is yours, not ours.'

The head accountant shut the door behind her. Love and all that nonsense! This Carol's spinning a yarn. Then the words came back to him, 'But what about me?'

'Shubhang,' he told himself, 'You're a very self-centred man. So what! Everyone is. Why change? You've done well for yourself! You have no one to worry about when you're dead and cremated…' The voice stopped. It was typical of him, miserly in his self-doubts as well. He couldn't change. Governance could change, but not him. Never.

He opened the cupboard, checked the stocks and debentures, the receipt of the bank locker. There was a sense of supreme satisfaction. Yet those words ricocheted, 'But what about me?'

Now there was someone else, a child.

Shubhang thought for a while about his lonely, cramped life. Then he left his room, caught the tram to Park Street and walked briskly to the florist's.

Carol was at the counter, bunching up roses. He walked up to her and said quietly, 'Please may I take my daughter home?'

An actor-turned-director, his storytelling craft discloses a New Age sensibility, taking in contemporary issues as in *Swades,* as well as travelling back to the past in the period epics *Lagaan, Jodhaa Akbar* and *Khelein Hum Jee Jaan Sey*. While working with the mainstream matrix, his style and sensibility are underscored by a distinct signature.

ASHUTOSH GOWARIKER

Disbelieve it or not

Every house tells a story, especially those lost in time. And Maharashtra's coastal belt is studded with them. Unaffected by the trappings of modernism and boxed-in architecture, the airy, khaki stone-walled, wooden-beamed homes resonate with unwritten history. They speak of another period, another era.

While shooting key portions of a film on a near-forgotten chapter of India's struggle for independence in one such stand-alone home—ages old, but strong—Raj was convinced that it was haunted. The film's fortnight-long shoot was progressing normally, but Raj, a senior assistant director, was behaving abnormally. He swore that after sunset, an elderly woman with unblinking eyes would stand in a corner watching every move of his attentively. No one else could see her. Only Raj could. Perhaps this woman's ghost wished to communicate only with him. The rest of the crew laughed it off. Raj possessed a third eye which they didn't, they jibed good-naturedly. Soon after dusk, the woman would show up, he would point towards her. For the actors, director RR Upadhyay and the technical crew, there was no one in any corner of the large, maze-like structure.

When Raj's hallucinations wouldn't end, there was cause for worry. This couldn't go on. The ghost in Raj's line of vision had become a joke. It was becoming unpleasant. Immediate consultation with a doctor—a psycho-analyst or a psychiatrist—appeared to be the only solution. Cut away from the city, naturally the barren location offered no such specialist. Upadhyay would have to wait to get him diagnosed…psychoanalysed, or ask him to quit work. Now that would be callous.

At the very least, Raj needed a serious talking to by the director whose films down the last decades had either been major successes or major failures...happens to all. Upadhyay checked with a general practitioner in Mumbai who suggested that Raj be sent to his clinic as soon as possible. Or if Raj volunteered to talk about the invisible spirit to Upadhyay, it would be easier to diagnose whether he was hallucinating… or… The doctor said the 'or' could mean anything, give him breathing space for now. Chances were that Raj would speak more candidly with Upadhyay whom he admired, than with a doctor whom he didn't know at all.

Around 10 p.m., the unit retired to the guest house, a ten-minute drive from the ages-old house. Upadhyay had requested Raj to drop by for a chat once he had finished dinner.

A tentative knock on the door and Raj entered looking guilty. 'I'm sorry,' he murmured. 'I don't know what's happening to me. If you like, I'll leave tomorrow morning.' Refusing to sit, he continued, 'If you don't mind, I'll stand.'

Strange that—why stand like a student before a school teacher?—but whatever made him feel at ease, his director would go with that.

'Please believe me, I'm not lying about this lady,' Raj said, avoiding eye contact with the director. He went on to describe the 'lady' as fiftyish, tall, and almost masculine. By masculine, he specified that she was large-boned, broad-shouldered and stood firm like a warrior before entering a battlefield. Strands of her crow-black hair, oiled and thick, fell on her considerable eyebrows. Exposure to sun had toughened her skin, now the texture of deep brown leather. Whenever she caught Raj's eye while he cued the actors, she smiled conspiratorially as if she had resolved to be visible exclusively to him.

Raj had never been this descriptive. His forte was camera movement, shot divisions and sync-sound recording. When it came to the script, he had never offered half an input. Now he was speaking as if he could write several scripts.

'The ghost...,' Raj sliced the sentence, 'is keeping a watch on me.' Suddenly, he slumped into a chair. He was sweating profusely. He looked around the room and then at the tree out of the window, illuminated by moonlight. He didn't say a word for the longest stretch of time.

Upadhyay, known for his brusqueness, congratulated himself for being patient. Sensing that the director would have to tell him to shape up or catch the next bus, train, or taxi out of the township, Raj said, 'I know you don't need this. I'm making an ass of myself. If I leave in the middle of the shoot, word will get around that I'm nuts. In this industry, just one bad word and a thousand rumours spread. There are just three days left. I'll pull myself together.'

Upadhyay assented with a nod which conveyed, 'Any more ghost business from you and you're out.'

Raj jumped up, smiled, 'And please don't think I'm into drugs or booze. I'm not denying that I like my two drinks before dinner—a beer or a vodka. I'm giving up on that. I'll be fine...'

'And if you're not?'

'I will be...my work won't suffer. Promise...God promise.'

The meeting with Raj ended on an inconclusive note. Frankly, the unit needed him. The continuity girl had demanded sudden leave of absence, the clapper boy was goofing up big time. Raj was indispensable for the next three days whether he was cuckoo or not.

The next day, he was perfect...till the last shot of the day was okayed. Raj yelled out victoriously, 'Did it, did it, did it. Didn't see her...didn't see the lady.' The rest of the unit pretended not to hear or see the brass amulet he was wearing. Probably his way of warding off evil. The fact was that the junior assistants liked Raj and rated him a guru. Mercifully, at the guest house, dinner was uneventful. He refused beer, giving the impression that he had attained sainthood.

In a film's unit, there can be as many as six to eight assistants or just a couple of them. Their work goes largely unpaid and unrecognised unless they find a break as solo directors. Rajan Kolhatkar, nicknamed Raj, had been approached to direct two or three projects on his own steam, but had turned them down on the grounds that they were 'rabidly commercial'. He wanted to be a cut above. A graduate from Pune's Film and Television Institute of India, his training in direction had been partly financed by a scholarship. He never talked about this, but his family comprised only his father and himself. His mother had passed away soon after giving birth to her first-born. The father was a clerk in the divisional collector's office in Satara, on the verge of retirement.

The house for the shoot had been sighted by Raj in the course of a bus ride between Mumbai and Satara. The forlorn structure had whizzed by, but had stayed in his memory. A recce later, it was hired for a fortnight for a sum settled by the district collector. The sum wasn't exactly a bargain, totalling ₹10 lakhs. The money would go to its owner's nephews settled in Nashik, besides clearing the debts owed by them to the collectorate.

The location, empty for miles and miles, was a shrub-land, spurting unwelcoming cactii, pariah dogs, and frequently visited by a school of parrots so green that they seemed like paint splattered on a dull canvas. When the shoot commenced, very few locals dropped by on cycles, with their children balanced precariously on the rusting top tubes. Unaccustomed to the tedium of a shoot, they stopped arriving after a couple of days, which is what any unit dreams of—to be left alone to do their work without interruption and autograph seekers. The locals didn't know what autographs were about, but they did know the leading actors, having watched their films' re-runs on television.

Without a doubt, a bond grows between a director and his assistants who become his generals on the camera field. Yet a certain distance has to be maintained, almost as a corporate rule—this far, no further. That's why Upadhyay didn't know much about his star assistant except the basics: the stocky, intense, techno-savvy Raj was unmarried, interacted with the female assistants in an avuncular manner, and aspired to direct movies with socialistic underpinnings. Beyond this, the director didn't need to know more.

After Raj's hallucinations began, his father had elaborated nervously over the phone, 'He wouldn't want me to disturb him at work, sir. I'm a poor, simple man. He would get embarrassed. No, he has never had such visions before. All I can say is that he has always felt the lack of a mother...he feels bad that she died while giving him birth. There was a time when he would keep crying, wishing he hadn't been born. I'm talking too much, sir. He won't like it. I beg you to please take care of him...he speaks very highly of you.'

Whether Upadhyay could accept that responsibility would have to be decided on the film unit's return to Mumbai. While a shoot is on, a director believes that there is nothing more important than the film he is making. Neither hail nor storm. In any case, there were only two more days to go. The schedule had gone clockwork. No delays, no glitches. Again, on the penultimate day, Raj was fine...till the December sun descended over the distant hillocks surrounding the house. Raj turned pale, chanted a mantra inaudibly and held on to his amulet. 'Sir, excuse me. Someone is calling me,' he whispered and bolted from the spot. Not done. But if Upadhyay had objected, the schedule would have been disrupted. 'Sort yourself out,' the director said. 'Go. I don't want any scenes here.'

At the guest house, Raj didn't show up for dinner. His colleagues said he wasn't in his room either. Outside, there was a downpour of unseasonal rain, lightning and thunderstorm which ended as suddenly as they had begun. Next, well past midnight, the collector called up the unit's online production executive to inform him that the house couldn't be used any more. Upadhyay, jolted out of his sleep, told the production executive, 'Rubbish! You're in charge of the production. Pay that collector...or whoever he is... if he wants money. This is blackmail... It's not possible to cheat the remaining shots elsewhere. We can't afford to... the budget will go haywire.'

The production executive connected Upadhyay to the collector. The collector's tone was placatory, 'Please understand.'

'I don't understand,' Upadhyay said, absolutely exasperated. 'Full payment has been made. What the hell is the problem? Do you want a bribe? Is that it? We have done that already. You guys are never satisfied.'

The collector didn't react to the insult. He said that he would reach the guest house at 7 a.m. and explain. 'Explain all you want,' Upadhyay retaliated firmly. 'I will not let my shooting get affected. I know the Chief Minister. I'll take the matter to him, if need be.'

'Sir, no need to threaten me. There's a problem. Hear me out...then it's up to you,' the collector ended.

Well before 7 a.m., the collector—surprisingly in his early thirties, neatly attired in a pair of jeans and a white tee—drove up alone to the guest house in a lumbering Ambassador car. He requested Upadhyay to sit with him in the car. The unit members shouldn't be within earshot. Upadhyay, at the end of a tether, sat in the car with the collector who looked as if he was about to reveal a military secret. According to his account, the old house with no name or number was haunted by the spirit of a woman whose three-month-old child had died soon after a bout of pneumonia. The woman was sitting with the child on the garden swing. The rains had poured down unseasonally. Despite her dashing into the house, the child was soaking wet. There was nothing untoward about the child's death. He had died of natural causes.

The woman, about 22 years old, was never the same again. She went into a shell. Her husband endured her silence for a couple of years, a bit more maybe, and brought in a second wife to the house. The woman walked out of the house, never to be seen again. It was rumoured that she had moved to another town, or she could have killed herself. There was no trace of her. Police investigations had drawn a blank.

As it happened, the house proved to be unlucky for the man and his second wife. A fire gutted a section of the house and they were roasted alive in their sleep.

Although the structure was repaired and renovated, for decades no one would buy the house or rent it. It was believed that the childless mother's ghost resided there. Whoever had entered it had felt an unbearable icy chill, and heard a woman mumbling, 'My son...my son...come back.' In fact, the collector and his staff were relieved when the film unit's work had progressed without any interference, supernatural or otherwise.

'Last night,' the collector went on with his tale, 'we suspect that your assistant was walking aimlessly on the highway when a speeding state transport bus hit him. The passengers, the bus driver and the conductor say he was covered in blood...must have suffered multiple fractures, but before he could be rushed to the hospital, he got up and said he was fine. He told them his name was Raj and that he was your assistant, but he had quit. 'Nothing can harm me, not even God,' he said this very proudly. He pointed towards the barren field across the highway and said that as long as his mother was with him, no harm could come to him. He glowed. There wasn't a speck of blood on him anymore.

'But where is Raj?' Upadhyay asked, not believing a word.

According to the bus driver, Raj had sprinted across the field. It was pitch dark, but in the moonlight, a woman carrying a brass *thali* could be seen. She applied a vermilion *tika* on his forehead as if he was on his way to a battlefield. They could hear her reciting a mantra in a high-pitched voice. Then it went totally dark, as if someone had switched off the moonlight. Raj and the woman had vanished.'

It was no point arguing with the collector. It would be the director's belief in the rational versus an absurd account by a busload of passengers at the police *chowki*.

Ever the pragmatist Upadhyay reasoned, 'Let's, for a minute, accept every word that you've told me as the truth. How does that prevent me from shooting in the house today? All I need is a few hours there. We'll wrap up fast.'

The collector responded, 'That is the strangest part. The house is in a shambles...it has collapsed...as if it was struck down by lightning.'

'What?'

'You can see for yourself. I came here so as not to alarm your unit. We don't want any kind of news to spread. There can be panic. The locals, as it is, are petrified of the place.'

What about the passengers who saw Raj and his 'mother' disappear? The collector was willing to take a chance on that, 'They don't know about the house. I'm told the passengers wanted to leave the place as soon as possible. They told themselves it was probably some movie stunt. And the driver was relieved that the man he had hit had walked away, unharmed. All that is under control. I would request you not to visit the location today, but it's for you to decide. And as for your allegations about bribes, I will ignore them. I can understand that this is a strange situation.'

Upadhyay understood the collector's logic. At a pinch, the remaining shots could be done in a studio. It wouldn't be the same, but then filmmaking is so frequently assailed by exigencies. The unit left the guest house by 10 a.m. Naturally everyone wondered about Raj's absence. 'Do you think he has gone back to Mumbai?' his colleagues asked with concern.

Raj's cell phone was switched off. His flatmate, a theatre actor, didn't know his whereabouts. Raj's father was anxious. He would call Upadhyay every day, 'Has my son returned? Where is he?'

After a year, the father stopped calling. There was no point. Who was to get into theories? A man who had never seen his mother. A woman who had lost her only child. They had adopted each other. 'Come on,' Upadhyay told himself, 'such a story would be lapped up in cinema, not in reality.'

Every little sign of the remnants of the house was erased. To date, Upadhyay is clueless. A sense of guilt lingers. Where can the hunt for Raj begin? Maybe he's alive, maybe not. Either way, RR Upadhyay would like to believe that Raj is with his mother, in whichever realm he is.

A prime force in the film society movement, he initiated his career in direction with the intimately scaled *Saara Akash,* swerving then towards comedies and love stories, ceaselessly radiating warmth towards the middle class. He has also made Bengali films. His most cherished films include *Rajnigandha, Chhoti Si Baat, Chitchor, Swami, Khatta Meetha* and *Shaukeen,* although he treasures the little-seen *Jeena Yahan* as his most accomplished work.

BASU CHATTERJI

The window

Suddenly, the window opened into a new world. From a hovel in a tumbledown *chawl,* they had shifted into a two-room-one-kitchen apartment. 450 square feet carpet area, which can be a palace for those who have subsisted, ever since they can remember, in fifty square feet or less.

Carpet? Not to be taken literally, it's just real-estate legalese. No carpets, rugs or *kilims* for them. Instead, they had spread out three or four bright-bordered mats bought after fierce haggling at the *chatai* market in Bhendi Bazaar.

For years, the lights had to be switched throughout the day in the room situated in the walled-in section of the *chawl* on Do Taanki, Agripada. Now, they were just getting used to the idea of sunshine speeding into their third-storey home which they could actually call an apartment. The address was nothing to be embarrassed about. It was in the heart of Parel, the city's industrial area where century-old mills were being demolished to give way to housing colonies for the upper middle class and also the swishier income groups.

Goodbye *chawl,* so airless that it was asphyxiating. Now, life was looking up...towards a butterscotch sun smiling from a crayon blue sky.

In fact, Rehana Muneer Malik and her two daughters were behaving as if they had moved into heaven. A window—a sliding sheet of glass encased in metal frames—was quite easily the most priceless treasure in a house which belonged to them. Imagine, their home was bought on ownership terms with stamp paper duty paid. All the complicated formalities were signed, sealed and acquired. The reversal of lifestyle, however modest, had been arranged by Rehana Begum's son who had one day—at long last—landed a job as a junior supervisor of a construction company in Dubai. Before that, the son was employed in Mumbai as a salesman in a stationery shop—underpaid and overworked.

The son had done it. The paragon of virtue had extricated his family from darkness which invariably exacerbates despair. The mother and his two sisters adored him unconditionally. They had wept as if the world was about to end the day he left hastily for the job organised by an employment broker. The passport, visa and air ticket (one-way) were rushed by his employers only a few hours before he hugged his mother and sisters tight to his heart. They were afraid he wouldn't ever return, that he would forget about them the instant he left home. He assured them that he would die before committing such a sin. Gratitude was ingrained in him by his parents from the day he was born. He would never miss reciting his prayers five times a day, and he would keep all the *rozas* during the month of Ramzan. Without him, life was inconceivable. He promised his mother that he would send a fair amount of money every month through a contact of his, who would hand it over to her personally. The cash received in envelopes promised a key to a house where they could breathe freely, and live without depending on an 80-watt electric bulb 24x365 days.

The money from Dubai was in four figures to start with, then five, topped by one with as many zeroes as it takes to complete the price for an apartment with a view. Rehana Begum was grateful, more to Allah than to her son who was only doing his duty by his family. Her husband, Muneer Syed Malik, a schoolteacher in Lucknow, had moved to Mumbai in the mid-1970s. He couldn't get along with his two elder brothers who ran a wholesale establishment of Lucknow *chikan kurtas*. It was felt he wasn't contributing sufficiently to the joint family's kitchen expenses. In any case, Mumbai was lored to be the city of better opportunities. Not true: the *madrasas* were overcrowded with teachers and naturally, the convent schools wouldn't entertain the notion of teaching Urdu studies. Not prescribed by the board, not needed. At most, Malik *miyan* could give tuitions in Urdu to two or three students, thrice a week. He earned a pittance.

To add insult to injury, Rehana Begum would taunt him, '*Miyan*, what is the use of knowing Urdu and *thodisi angrezi*, if it can't earn you a decent living? I'm telling you even now…it's not too late…let's return to Lucknow.' Malik *miyan* fretted, but could do little for his two children and one more on the way. When he passed away without warning in his sleep, the widow felt abandoned, 'Now look what you've done. Is this a joke? Leaving me with mouths to feed, just like that!'

She couldn't return to Lucknow. Without Malik *miyan,* Rehana Begum wouldn't be welcomed by his brothers and sisters-in-law. They would let her stay for a week, a month, a year maybe. Then what? She chose to cling on to her pride, found employment as a part-time cleaner, sweeper, cook. The newborn she would leave in a crèche or in the *chawl* with a friend who would ask for a little payment at the end of the month. Her son and daughter went to the municipal school and even managed to clear their SSC examinations. The youngest daughter was extra-bright and precocious, but was shunted into a school that was run by a group of Muslim philanthropists.

Although Malik *miyan* thought that his *humnasheen,* Rehana Begum, was eccentric, he didn't object when she named her first-born Azghar and their daughter Azadeh. She liked the first letter in the alphabet. 'If their names start with the letter "A", they will prove to be A-1 in their lives,' she felt. Malik *miyan* had grunted, 'What's in a name? As you like it,' pleased as punch by his mixed Shakespeare allusion. The Maliks' second daughter, born two months after *miyan*'s death, was named Azra. So that was it.

Although, she cleaned and swabbed, she retained her self-given title of Begum. Her late husband would be remembered as '*miyan*'. '*Saab*' sounded much too servile.

When Rehana Begum and her two daughters relocated, a semblance of stability was achieved. The widow, now pushing fifty-five, didn't have to carry out menial chores anymore.

Azadeh, all of twenty-five, worked as an accountant at an Urdu bookshop, and attended morning classes in French at the Alliance Française: French because she nurtured a desire to visit Paris. And who knows? Maybe she would find the man of her dreams there, right under the Eiffel Tower? At times, Azadeh dreamt in French.

Azra, younger than her *badi aapa* by nearly ten years, studied at an affordable school, commuting to and fro by bus. And the hero of the family, Azghar, was twenty-eight, the age which his mother proclaimed, 'is so right for a boy's marriage in today's society, but poor Azhu, he has sacrificed his happiness so that we can lead a decent life. You girls, always remember that.' Azadeh and Azra didn't need such reminders, they prayed for their brother's well-being every day. Azghar's portrait, clicked by Azadeh at an amusement park, was neatly mounted and framed, and nailed on the drawing room's wall.

Conventionally, Rehana Begum would not have allowed any pictures on the walls, but beliefs could be relaxed for Azghar. If it were not for him, they would have died in that miserable *chawl*, and she would have had to clean, sweep and scrub till her back gave way. It nearly had.

Every Sunday, the daughters took turns to apply Tiger balm to her developing hunch. 'My back is collapsing my dear girls,' she would whinge, 'I'm just a guest on this earth till Allah summons me. I only want to see my Azhu before I die. It's been years since he has gone to that Dubai place…he could come and see us for a few days, but work is work, I suppose.' The dutiful son did call occasionally, a two-minute conversation over a foggy cellphone that would leave his mother and sisters pleading for more. *Bade bhai* always thought of others, never about himself.

Neither too tall nor short, the olive-complexioned Azhgar wore spectacles, had thick, silken hair, and a perfect smile except for the chipped front tooth. He had been hit by a hockey stick on the *maidan* while playing for an inter-school match. He never had an evening fuzz on his face and needed to shave only twice a week. His voice, always at a low volume, reminded Rehana Begum of her Malik *miyan*. She adored her *miyan* when he talked gently, almost apologetically, when he wished to make love once the children were asleep. The girls inherited their looks from their mother, serene yet fiery when provoked. Both possessed light dimples, flowing chocolate brown hair, braided, which they weren't allowed to trim or cut. Azadeh and Azra were beauties and knew it. This brought a touch of *hauteur* to their personalities. Not surprisingly, Azadeh had turned down dozens of marriage proposals from Muslim families who belonged to the upper-middle-class income bracket. 'I was just 18 when I married Malik *miyan*,' the mother would nag her daughter. 'Whom are you waiting for? A prince to drop down from heaven? Child, you have to leave us some day.' Azadeh would hug her mother, taking care to avoid the incipient hunch and kiss her face sloppily, '*Ammi*, I'll never get married. I want to be with you always...and always.'

Azra, the precocious one would intervene, '*Baaji* is a liar. She'll leave us as soon as she finds a Frenchman, *n'est-ce pas, ma soeur?*" And *baaji* would retort, '*Tais-toi, paagal ladki*.' The two would get into Frenchindi, and *baaji* would taunt her, '*Pehle* learn English...you get such terrible marks!' Azra would crow, 'Not so terrible, *baaji* I top my class every year, don't I?'

Rehana Begum would leave them bickering, whingeing, 'Instead of arguing, how about helping me out in the kitchen, you hopeless things?' Invariably the girls would retreat to their bedroom or switch on TV, to a soap about mean mums-in-law, if only to see which of their victims was wearing the most blingy sari. Once, Azra had remarked casually, '*Baaji,* I hope your *saas* isn't ever so horrid to you, but at least you'll be wearing wonderful saris after you get married. No?' Their wardrobe was restricted to cotton *salwar kameez*es and voluminous *dupattas*. On Eid, they would be dressed more vibrantly in rosebud-printed polyesters.

Months, then over a year, elapsed. The window in their bedroom overlooked an endless slum. The mother's room looked into the building's compound, a parking site for the residents' EMI-facilitated cars, as well as motorbikes and cycles. The sisters aspired to own a 'family' car in the near future. They just had to ask *bhaijaan* and he would send them the cash, but they didn't want to be greedy. Why, now they even had their own toilet with a geyser. Gone were those mornings of queuing up before the *chawl*'s common toilet where they would dash in and out, pinching their noses to avoid the vaporous stink.

On Sundays, Azadeh and Azra invented a sport which could be played without leaving home. From the drawing room's large window, baked by sunshine, the sisters people-watched. Two tall peepul trees bookended the view of the narrow backlane.

Bang opposite, was another housing colony. Its ground floor occupied by a high-priced gelato ice-cream outlet attracted a few customers. Next to it, Super Lucky Provision Stores did brisk business throughout the week, especially on Sundays. A hole-in-the-wall laundry, affected by discounted rates of washing machines at the malls was on its last legs.

The provision store with its sacks of wheat, sugar and *daals*, and home essentials, was a veritable carnival. Azra's eyes would be trained on its roly-poly owner, Mulji *bhai*, raining abuses on his retinue of salesmen, but fondly: '*Saala chutiye* log, work properly or I'll cut your salary.' Then he would console them, 'Dear boys, I am like your father. And fathers are entitled to give *gaalis*.' The sales boys would smile as if they had been adopted on the spot. Besides the portly Mulji *bhai*, the girls would be amused by idle strollers, more often than not accompanied by dogs on leashes. Azra's favourite was a Great Dane who would spray the lampost with a waterfall of urine as if it was playing target practice.

Then Azra saw someone better. A man with movie star good looks: gym-sculpted, his muscles outlined sharply against his white short-sleeved shirt, a pair of narrow powder-blue jeans, calf-leather boots and Ray-Ban glares. Ruddy-complexioned, and swinging stylishly off his Royal Enfield bike, his cleft chin could be seen even from the window. He was lighting a cigarette with a Zippo the first time Azra sighted him, and called out to Azadeh, '*Baaji*. Come, come fast. *Ek* hero *aaya hai*.'

Mulji *bhai* greeted the man effusively, but requested him to stub out the cigarette, 'There's kerosene around. You want us to go up in smoke?' The mobike rider crushed the cigarette under his boot, put his arm familiarly around Mulji *bhai.* At the counter, Mulji *bhai* and the man talked for a long time. A medium-sized van arrived, delivering crates of the new cola drink which was being advertised all over town. Stylishly, the man saluted Mulji *bhai,* got him to sign on a paper, nodded to the van's driver, and zoomed off. Captivated, the kid sister watched every little move of his.

Azra jumped off the high stool, '*Baaji,* this is the man for you.' Azadeh, who stood still at the window, slapped her lightly on the cheek. 'You say anything that comes to the silly little head of yours, don't you?"

'He's sooo good-looking,' the kid sister said. 'If I was old enough, I would marry him.'

'Stupid. Shut up. Don't let *ammi* hear you. You don't want to taste her anger, do you?"

'But she's never angry, *baaji.*'

'Don't you ever make her angry. Understand?'

'Understand, understand.'

The sisters returned to mean mothers-in-law-watching on the tube.

Azra would catch sight of the young man on Wednesday, then Friday, practically every alternate evening. She'd call out to Azadeh, 'He's here, he's here.' Most days, the sisters would stand transfixed till one day Rehana Begum joined them at the window, 'What are you two up to? Glued here! Is there some ninth wonder of the world you can see from here? I want to see it also...'

Azadeh said cleverly, '*Ammi*, we like to see the dog troubling his owner. He won't budge after he has...relieved himself. It's funny, very funny.'

Rehana Begum saw the dog who was looking expressionlessly at the strollers. The Dane's owner was pleading, 'Come on now, come come...good boy good boy,' till he silenced her with a bark as if to say, 'Go to hell, lady.'

'What's so funny?' the mother wondered. 'All dogs are like this.'

'No, no,' Azra giggled. 'They're supposed to be a man's best friend.'

The hero was still getting the cola crates unloaded. The sisters gaped at him. This Sunday, he wore a lime-green T-shirt over black linen trousers. His hair was gelled. He was sneaking a smoke since Mulji *bhai*'s back was turned while taking stock of the delivery. Then came the big moment. The man looked up towards the window. His gaze stuck on Azra who panicked, '*Aapa*, he's looking at me!' Instinctively, Azra waved out to him. He waved back. Oh, oh, oh. Azra jumped off the high stool. Azadeh closed the window, and hissed, 'Are you mad? What will he think of us? He's a stranger.'

'But I like him. I want him for you. I'll be so happy to see you on that bike. You'll let me go on rides with him also, no? You won't be jealous, *na*?'

Azadeh looks extremely upset, but was thrilled with the idea of a match made at a heavenly window. Azra stoked her feelings, 'So handsome! He's the handsomest man I've ever seen.'

"*Chal hut*, our Azghar *bhai* is more handsome.'

Azra, after a pause, conceded, 'Yes, yes, *bhaijaan* is a rockstar. The best!'

The man's deliveries to the provision store became a daily ritual. Azra and Azadeh watched him, lit by the glorious evening light. And he would look up at the window. First he would smile at Azadeh who would turn her face away. Then he would wave at Azra who would return the wave happily, without any self-censorship. But it was time to investigate who this dude was, and if all his qualities met her expectations, she would play Cupid. 'You are cordially invited to the *nikaah* of Azadeh Muneer Malik and Hot Hunky Dude,' she was already planning the wedding ceremony, and the honeymoon. If he was rich enough—and he did look sufficiently posh—they would fly off to Paris and send Azra a postcard from the Eiffel Tower. *Très romantique.*

Azra's load of homework on Wednesdays was heavy. Still, writing an essay, learning history dates by rote and figuring out the various capitals of the world had to be put on hold. The hunk had arrived. Azra could tell from the sputter of the motorbike. Azadeh hadn't returned yet and *ammi* was chatting with the next-door neighbour, an ancient and infirm crone given to concocting gossip about the entire neighbourhood.

Azra ran down the three flights of stairs out of breath and pretended to be composed and cool at the Super Lucky Provisions Store. She asked Mulji *bhai* for a set of pencils, rejecting the ones she actually needed. Hunky Dude was around, talking to the boys about the rising sales of the colas. She pretended not to notice him when his hand landed on her shoulder. This was scary. Had he detected her mission:

investigation? Apparently he hadn't. He asked for a cola from the store's ice box to be handed over to Azra, then turned to face her, 'Have you tried this drink yet?'

Azra had, but shook her head. 'You'll like it,' he said seriously. 'I will be upset if you don't take it. I will feel insulted.'

Azra hung on to the iced bottle as if it was a slimy serpent. She inquired haughtily, 'So, gentleman, what is your name? What do you do? Where do you live? Why do you wave out to me...and look at...,' she stopped, aware that she was blabbering.

'Aaah, how about telling me your name first?' he asked sweetly.

'Azra, Azra Muneer Malik.'

'And the lady's..?'

'She's my sister. Azadeh, Azadeh Muneer Malik...best sister in the world. All right then. I'm leaving," Azra said, hoping he would ask her to stay.

'Oh, oh, such a fiery temper. Okay, *baba*, okay. I'm Zafar Ali, Assistant Manager at the factory which manufactures the drink you're holding, but not drinking.'

Azra downed some nervously. Zafar was enjoying this, 'I stay in Bandra. I wave to you because I want to be your friend. And I look at the other lady because she's beautiful.'

Surprisingly, Azra looked crestfallen. Zafar added suavely, 'Both of you are beautiful.'

Consoled, Azra perked up, 'So you are Muslim!'

'Yes. You have any problems with that? Next you'll want to know if I'm married and how many children I have!'

'Yes. How did you know?'

'Because any intelligent little girl would want to know a stranger's background before waving out to him again.'

'Right. Are you married?'

'No, I'm not married.'

'Any children?'

He laughed out loud. Azra realised her line of questioning had gone stupidly wrong. She laughed with him, to which he said, 'Friends?'

'Friends.'

'Pukka?'

'200 per cent pukka!'

'Then will you do one thing? Give my *salaams* to that beautiful girl who's at the window with you.'

'I will do that,' Azra drank down the cola as fast as she could. 'It's good. I drink it whenever I can.'

'But you said you've never had it.'

Azra blushed, 'I'll give *aapa* your *salaams*. *Khuda haafiz.*'

'*Khuda haafiz.*'

Aapa Azadeh feigned indifference. Next day, she went to the extent of veiling the window with a thin lace white curtain, perfect for the sun to light the room gently.

'But why?' Azra asked with concern. 'It only comes in our way...'

'In our way of what, Azra dear?'

'*Aapa,* we'll have to draw it apart every time we are at the window...'

'Good, gives us the option of privacy...if we want it.'

The seed had been planted. Azadeh may have attached the curtains to the windows pelmet, but drew it apart with a flourish when it was the hour of Zafar-watching. He never failed to look up and now cupped his hands into a *salaam*. One evening, with a wave of the hand, he asked Azra to come down right away. He gave her two tickets for the night show of a movie at a nearby multiplex. He would join them there. Love was in the air. The little sister was excited, but would *aapa* agree to come? Would their mother grant them permission to go out after dinner? Quite easily done. Rehana Begum was told that they were being accompanied by a friend and their parents, nothing to worry about. They would clock in before midnight.

'How about taking me along?' the mother suggested tentatively.

Nope, sorry. There were no more tickets to be bought for love or money. She could always catch up on the film when it would be telecast.

Zafar was the epitome of charm, insisting that they should have a fun time, complete with caramel popcorn, nachos dipped in tangy sauce and cold coffee. Azra sat in between Azadeh and Zafar, but changed her seat during the intermission. Neither objected. A little after the house lights went down, Azra saw that Zafar's hand was tantalisingly close to her sister's. The movie was a blank screen. Who cared what went on up there? The blossoming romance was much more exciting. Azra closed her eyes, 'I hope they hold hands, I hope, I hope...' They did, lingering behind the kid sister during the silent walk back home. She likes him, she likes him not, no no, she likes him very much. He liked her very much too, throwing away his packet of cigarettes dramatically when Azadeh asked petulantly, 'Must you smoke?'

A month went by in romantic slow-motion. Zafar and Aazdeh would meet at parks, malls and the same multiplex to see the same film over and over again. One night, Azra asked her sister point-blank, 'Has he kissed you?'

'Shut up! You say anything that comes into your silly head.'

'Come on *aapa*. I won't tell *ammi*. Please, please, please... has he?'

'Maybe, maybe not.'

Azra hugged Azadeh, 'Wow, you lucky thing...he's so cool.'

A pause, and then Azadeh confessed, 'But I don't know if he's serious about me. I don't want to get hurt...or *ammi* to find out. She'll kill me.'

'She won't. And of course he's serious. He loves you. I'm sure of that.'

'How do you know that?'

'Oh, we girls always know...'

'How you talk! As if you're an expert.'

'Just you wait. I'll find out.'

'How?'

'Wait *na*...'

Next day, Azra bolted down the stairs as soon as she saw Zafar from the window. When Mulji *bhai* was serving some customers, she asked, 'You love my sister, don't you?'

Zafar laughed out loud, 'Of course I do. Why? Has your *aapa* said something?'

'She has said nothing. I wanted to make sure you're serious about her.'

'How you talk!' he patted her head. 'I am very serious. I would like to marry her.'

'When?'

'As soon as she agrees. I'll come and meet your mother on Sunday...to ask for her hand.'

'Promise! *Khaao kasam.*'

'*Teri kasam,* my little imp.'

Azra sped to the apartment, announced the news to Azadeh, who was unsure, 'What about *ammi?* She's not going to like this.'

'No one can *not* like Zafar *bhai,* and you know that!'

'I hope you're right. I don't know...am I doing the right thing?'

'Do you want to marry one of those weirdo guys arranged by *ammi,* or what?'

'No. But how do I...we, tell her?'

'Leave it to me.'

'No,' Azadeh squealed. 'I'll tell Khurshedi *khatoon* and ask her to talk to *ammi.*'

'What if she messes it up?'

'We'll have to take that risk, Azra. We can't talk to *ammi... chhoti moonh aur badi baat.*'

'What on earth is that, *aapa?*'

'You don't know anything.'

'*Chhoti moonh...*small mouth!' Azra decoded the phrase. '*Aur badi baat...*and big talk!'

'Exactly!'

The building's know-all Khurshedi *khatoon* heard out Azadeh attentively, chagrined that she hadn't scented a love story which had the right ingredients for a scandal with her ability for grinding *masala* out of thin air. Her forehead deeply furrowed, she expressed her doubts as soon as Azadeh's shy narration was over.

Hauling herself from her double-mattressed bed, the arthritis-ridden Khurshedi hobbled to the kitchen, poured black tea from a blacker kettle, plonked a couple of sugar cubes into a mug and returned to squat on the mattress. She declared imperiously, 'Child. I don't have a good feeling about what you've just told me. If this man has been at Mulji *bhai*'s for so many months, why hasn't he ever come up to meet Rehana and inform her about his intentions? Sounds shady. Who knows where he's from? Have you met his parents? Does he have brothers and sisters? Have you checked how he lives…and where?'

'Yes, of course,' Azadeh lowered her head shyly, lying through her teeth. She knew nothing about Zafar except that they loved each other. If he was older than her by ten years, she didn't care. Khurshedi *khatoon* could sense that Zafar would have to be given a chance. He would have to be grilled.

The very same day, Zafar reached the Maliks' apartment on the dot of 6.30. Rehana Begum who still had to digest the news of her daughter's secret romance, was ready to give battle, but melted at first sight of her prospective son-in-law. As soon as the man, dressed in a light jacket, entered the house, he said '*Salaam valeikum*' with '*Adaab*', and by turn bent to touch the feet of Rehana Begum and Khurshedi *khatoon*. He placed two gift-wrapped boxes of chocolate before them, 'Sweets for the two sweet ladies.'

Rehana Begum scanned him. This man was sincere, well-mannered and handsome. Khurshedi *khatoon* wasn't impressed, and said in a voice of pure steel, 'Zafar, you should have brought some elders from home. It isn't right for you to come like this and ask for our Azadeh as if she's another chocolate box in a shop.'

Azadeh and Azra, monitoring the interview from a studied distance, winced. Khurshedi *khatoon* was being unnecessarily aggressive. Zafar darted an affectionate glance at Azadeh, and said, 'I understand completely. My father is no more. He passed away when I was ten or so. My mother raised me with much difficulty. She lives in Hyderabad with my sister, her husband and their children. She cannot walk easily. Arthritis, you know. She moves around with the help of a walking stick.'

Khurshedi *khatoon* softened, 'It must be very difficult for her, like it is for me.'

After this, Zafar sailed through.

Rehana Begum served tea with a variety of cream biscuits. The two inquisitors approved of the fact that Zafar was self-made, earned a monthly pay packet which was just short of ₹1 lakh after taxes, owned a 700-square feet home in Andheri, close to the factory where he was employed. They were also quite pleased that he had snagged a job with a multi-national company in America. If he hadn't accepted the offer, it was because he wanted to marry first, take his wife along...and at this point, he paused, '*Gustakhi maaf,* that is why we would like to get married as soon as we have your blessings.'

'But you are ten years older than our child,' Khurshedi *khatoon* returned to playing spoilsport.

Rehana Begum shushed her up sharply, 'So what! I was also 10...maybe 11 years younger than *miyan*...*beta* all I want is my child to be happy.'

'Are you expecting a dowry?' Khurshedi *khatoon* peered into his eyes.

'Allah forbid!' Zafar said, affronted. 'In fact, I would insist on giving a *meher* of ₹50 lakhs...'

It was a deal made in heaven. Zafar's mother, sister, her husband and their children would arrive from Hyderabad a few days before the *nikaah* which would be short and simple. The date was about to be set when Rehana Begum asked for reprieve, 'I'll need some time. Their brother must be here. Azghar is much too busy.'

Khurshedi *khatoon,* addicted to taking the contra-view, said, 'Then they might have to wait for an eternity. What if your Azghar can't get away for two to three years? Will you keep waiting for him till doomsday? If it's *chatt mangni patt shaadi,* so be it. He's their brother. Family comes above work. Azghar is a sensible boy. He'll be here.'

Within a fortnight, the *qaazi,* the auspicious hour, the wedding reception, were discussed and finalised. Azadeh's trousseau was in order. A smart *sherwani* and *churidar* was custom-made for Zafar. Azra ooh-ed when he tried it on to check the fit at the tailors, 'Zafar *bhai,* if I was older, I would have married you.'

'Oh, you can still marry me,' Zafar flirted.

'*Na*,' she clucked. 'You're not all that handsome. Wait till you see Azghar *bhai*.'

Azghar had secured two days leave and would be in Mumbai for the *nikaah*. He wouldn't be able to stay for the reception. Rehana Begum was disappointed, but elated at the thought of seeing him for a brief while at least.

After the reception, Azadeh and Zafar would take off for a honeymoon to the Maldives. 'And I'll be left all alone,' Azra pouted and ticked off her *aapa*. 'You don't care what happens to me, but I'll show you. Some day my honeymoon will be in Paris…and you won't like that, will you?'

'Shhh,' Azra knitted her eyebrows. 'Zafar is seeing if he can get some discounts…and change the tickets to Paris.'

'Ooooooh. *Bella bella*…'

'That's Italian, stupid.'

'Whaaat…ever.'

Three days before the *nikaah*, Zafar arrived at the apartment, looking unusually rattled, 'There's a problem. My mother and sisters do not approve…they say they will boycott me from the family. They cannot accept the fact that a Shia…is marrying a Sunni girl. I don't want to tell you what else they said…'

Rehana Begum wasn't startled. She was composed, 'I guess they want dowry.'

'Yes.'

'We are not in any position to offer you money,' she said firmly. 'My daughter, her clothes and a little jewellery are all I have been able to arrange. Their brother cannot do anything more.'

'I am not in favour of any dowry, *ammijaan*, but..'

'But...?'

'My family will not participate in the *nikaah*. That's fine by me. I don't care what my mother and sisters say. I'm willing to cut off all ties with them, if need be...'

'I cannot influence your decision. It's up to you.'

'The decision has been taken. I was only afraid that you might disapprove of my family's attitude.'

'Maybe they will relent some day.'

'*Inshallah*.'

'*Inshallah*.'

Anyone glancing through the window a night before the *nikaah* would have seen Rehana Begum waiting at the window. Azghar hadn't arrived by the late flight yet. The moment he reached home, she wouldn't let go of him, the girls would have to tear him away from her. She was certain that Azghar would look leaner, overworked, but at least he would be there, right before her eyes. There were so much to talk about, so much to thank him for. She hoped that he would bring a little diamond pendant for the bride, platinum cuff-links for the groom, yards of fabrics for his *ammi* and a Smartphone for Azra who would grab it, checking it right away for its game applications and camera megapixels.

Anyone who had kept looking at the drawing room in the apartment would have seen Rehana Begum continue to keep vigil at the window till it was daybreak. A little past 4 a.m. Her daughters would, then, lead her to the bedroom to catch some sleep. Azghar's flight must have been delayed. Azra would call the airlines, if she could get through, and inquire about its arrival status.

The *nikaah* was just a few hours away. Rehana Begum told the girls to switch off the lights, and grab some sleep.

At 7.30 a.m., Khurshedi *khatoon* rang the doorbell impatiently and lunged towards the TV set. She surfed the channels madly till she stopped at one of the 24-hour news programmes. She shouted at the top of her voice, 'See, see...just see...'

A two-minute capsule news report announced, 'Azghar Muneer Malik aka Chikna Babu, suspected by the police for complicity in the 26/11 bomb blasts was arrested on landing at the Sahar international airport early this morning. According to the police, after facilitating ammunition transfer as well as landing facilities for the terrorists, he had left the country a week before the attacks which took untold lives. His arrest was effected after a plan laid out by Crime Branch officer Saagar Singh Rathod. We will be back with more details shortly...'

Details? Rehana Begum didn't want to wait for them. The TV report showed her son being dragged into a jeep by constables. He attempted to cover his face. In vain. The constables dragged him through a melee of reporters and an enraged crowd at the airport. That visual byte was followed by a passport-sized photograph of Saagar Singh Rathod, the hero of the day.

Saagar Singh Rathod, Assistant Commissioner of Police, Crime Branch, had assumed the identity of Zafar Ali.

Anyone still looking at the window, would have seen Rehana Begum slump into Khurshedi *khatoon*'s arms. She was numb...unable to weep. Azra was crying, 'All this must be a mistake...'

A year later, Azadeh returned to her job at the bookshop. Its owner insisted she should. She wasn't to blame. She didn't ever return to the Alliance Française for lessons. She forgot Paris.

Ostracised at school, Azra bravely accepted the barbs which would be hurled at her. Then the barbs stopped. Then Rehana Begum stopped praying; she didn't feel the need to. Allah had been unfair to her. After all, she had never done anyone harm. She had been a good wife, a good mother, a staunch believer of the faith. So, why?

If only Azadeh and Azra had kept away from that window.

The quintessential B-town hero has incarnated the tender-hearted lover boy as well as the vengeful man of steel, endearing himself to young audiences of the 1990s, with *Barsaat, Gupt, Soldier* and *Ajnabee*. Of late, he has teamed up with his elder brother Sunny Deol and their father, the stalwart Dharmendra, in the *Yamla Pagla Deewana* franchise.

BOBBY DEOL

When the rains came

We didn't have to carry our problems—minor or major—on our shoulders. Bhag Singh did, he was protective about our family, never spoke about his own. For him, the Deols meant the inception and the closure of the world. His presence in our home guaranteed that nothing could go wrong, we could combat hail or storm with him on our team.

That's why my father never gave him a designation, Bhag Singh wasn't his secretary nor his troubleshooter. He was his shadow, and the extended family's security blanket. We'd call him Uncle, sir, *bhai*. He pronounced father's name as 'Dharmendarrra', in his quintessential Punjabi twang, his voice would rise quite a few decibels when he spoke of Dad—particularly when he answered the phone. He was as proud of him as a father would be of a child who has become an actor, a star, a hero. This pride he continued to feel for Sunny *bhaiyya* and then, for me, the kids he had cradled in his arms, spoken to in baby prattle, and who had never grown up in his eyes, even when we became parents ourselves. The way he had seen Dad in us, he saw us in our children.

A post-graduate in English literature, and an admirer of Sahir Ludhianvi's poetry, he would quote the angst-laden 'To be or not to be…' soliloquy of Hamlet, and Ludhianvi's words on the futility of violence. I would find it strange that he should recite it to me, since I had no talent at all for appreciating the worth of words. He'd catch me looking indifferent, but continue to recite Ludhianvi's plea for pacifism in a world torn by strife and bloodshed. The opening of the poem goes:

Zulm phir zulm hai, barat-ta hai to mitt jata hai
Khoon phir khoon hai, tapke ga to jum jayega

Khak-i-Sehra pe jumey yaa kaf-e-qatil pe jumey
Firq-e-insaaf pe yaa pai-e-silasal pe jumey
Taigh-i-baydad pe, yaa lash-e-bismil pe jumey
Khoon phir khoon hai, tapke ga to jum jayega

(Repression is still repression, rising it must flop
Blood is still blood, spilling it must clot

Whether it clots on desert sands, or upon assassins' hands
On justice's head or around shackled feet, on injustice's sword or on the wounded corpse
Blood is still blood, spilling it must clot)

Notes with couplets and proverbs he would keep in his desk at the office, situated on the ground floor of our home. They're still there, no one has dared to touch his books, diaries and letters. Under the glass top of the large desk, he had glued a typewritten sheet of emergency phone numbers: the fire brigade, the police, the ambulance service and the hospitals closest to our home in the Juhu-Vile Parle scheme. The phone numbers may have changed, but no one has replaced the typewritten sheet.

Sentimentality doesn't apply in my relationship with Bhag Singh. It was an emotional and grateful-to-one's-elder connect. Anyone who knew him identified him as a character—of strong moral values and loyalty, the sort they don't make anymore. His story was perhaps not very different from the scores of young men who arrived in Mumbai, back in the 1960s, dreaming of an entry into the film world. Tall, ruddy-complexioned with aquiline features, perhaps he wished to become an actor, but gained admission to the studios as a production manager with Darshan Sabharwal, then Ram Maheshwary, before joining my father as his secretary. From a township situated between Amritsar and Chandigarh, he found his niche in our home. He was aware that he would never be asked to reliquish his post, and even if we did, he would refuse to go.

After strategising Dad's career, it was natural that he should guide me through the thickets of film production, contracts, salaries, and handled our work diaries with unfailing precision. Additional staff had to be taken on, but he didn't complain of any intrusion on his beat. Every morning, when he was nearing the age of seventy, he'd walk miles from his room to our home, his double-in-one trick to avoid public transport and clock up his daily exercise too. He was perfectly fit and agile, till the date which is remembered by every Mumbaikar—July 26, 2005.

After the usual cloudbursts of the month, the day had begun normally with a steady rhythm of rainfall. The monsoon, when it does set in over the city, is a blessing. The lake levels report a rise, the weather bureau charts the figures—an alarming shortfall and a reassuring overflow alternately. There's a sense of comfort in the city when the rains don't end up playing truant. In the event, there won't be water cuts for the rest of the year. It wasn't dark as night at all, right till early afternoon. Then there was no respite, the rains didn't abate, the lights had to be switched on. It continued to rain, fast and furiously, as if the city had invoked the wrath of the gods. The skies kept turning black, schools shut down, film shoots at outdoor locations came to a halt abruptly. Studios shut shop. In front of the narrow road outside our home, the water level began to rise threateningly. It was flooded to a waist-knee height. And then higher. The cars parked out on the street and in our portico, were about to be submerged.

Television reports were predicting the worst—train services out of gear, public transport crippled, power breakdowns in innumerable pockets of the city. Fortuitously, at home there was no cause for panic. Everyone was indoors, dry, but impatient. Would the rains allow us to return to the studios the next day? Would the kids go to school? Was there sufficient food at home to last out two-three days? By some weather pattern or celestial diktat, practically every year sees a rough spell bordering on a deluge. It was getting there, with an ominous force which had not been witnessed in waking memory.

Bhag Singh, at his desk, was fretful. It took some persuasion to convince him that he would have to spend the night at our home, there was no way he could get a cab. No one could drive him home either, even in an SUV which couldn't have negotiated the mounting flood. He finally agreed to stay put in the office, or take the sofa in the drawing room, but he was visibly upset. He didn't express it in words, but his face said, 'I don't want to overstay my welcome. My duty compels me to leave the family to their privacy.'

Midnight set in, the house went quiet except for the rain lashes and rumbling thunder. And that's when we heard him collapse, with a faint scream. He had suffered a cardiac seizure, and was unconscious.

No doctor could be called, the phone lines were dead, cellphone networks were redundant. Bhag Singh had to be rushed to hospital that very moment, to Arogya Nidhi Hospital which is a five-minute walk away from our home. Easier thought than achieved. There was no time to revive him any which way or give him some medication at home. That could have worsened his condition. Dad rushed down from his room on the second storey of the house. Sunny *bhaiyya* and I followed. There was no time to waste. Our immediate next-door neighbour, we remembered, had an inflatable rubber raft in which his children played, pretending to be on high sea. *Bhaiyya* asked for the raft, Bhag Singh was placed on it, and Dad began his rescue operation.

I saw Dad, unflinchingly single-minded. He had to get the man who had been by his side for decades, to hospital. Ironically, all the emergency phone numbers maintained by Bhag Singh on the typewritten sheet under his desk's glass-top were of no use. By the time an ambulance arrived, if it did at all, it would have been too late.

The rains were getting nastier, unsparing in their assault. Since we knew how to swim, we piloted the raft through the flood which had reached a near-oceanic height by now. The rain stung. I can't recall every detail, but we managed to protect the man who had been our protector, to a degree with an umbrella held above him. We hoped that he wouldn't notice what was happening; that would only have embarrassed him. His pulse was weakening. Our speed was hampered by the flood which almost stonewalled us at points. Although good Samaritans, people who emerged from their temporary shelters, jumped into the water to help us, it took more than two hours to reach Arogya Nidhi.

The hospital was already overcrowded with people seeking medical attention (leeches had attacked the exposed skin of many of those who had tried to wade through the swirling waters). We picked up Bhag Singh from the raft as carefully as we could, and Dad pleaded for a doctor to attend to him as soon as it was humanly possible. I couldn't help remembering that when I was just out of infancy, Dad had raced down the streets to get me to hospital. The rest of the family was out at Chandan cinema; I had fallen from the first-floor balcony and was howling in pain. There were no cars at home. Dad hadn't thought twice, he had carried his child and run madly through the streets. That day Dad had saved his son. On July 26, he saved the man whom we had given the status of a brother, without saying it in so many words.

Bhag Singh survived the ordeal, but he was never the same again. After a month's recuperation, he was back, somewhat withdrawn, dressed in his customary pair of light blue jeans and a tucked-in long-sleeved striped shirt. With time, he regained the spring in his step, and the booming voice over the phone which now had an added 'don't-you-mess-with-me' timbre. Slowly, but surely, he resumed his long walks and was back in shape and good humour. Nearly 500 lives had been lost on the day of the deluge. He would laugh, 'I could have been No. 501. But my heroes kept me alive.' Dad would laugh, tell him not to talk morbidly, and not to describe any of us as heroes, saying, 'Heroism we do in the movies, not in real life, Bhag.'

Nearly seven years later, I had gone for an overseas shoot. On returning I missed Bhag's voice booming away in the office. Dad said he had asked for leave to be with his nephews in his hometown between Chandigarh and Amritsar. He never returned after that.

We kept in touch regularly, we would travel to his hometown to join in the wedding celebrations of his extended family.

He called on my birthday to wish me. When I asked him how he was, he said, 'I don't want to live any more.'

'Don't say such things, please,' I implored. That was the last time I heard his ever-familiar voice.

A few weeks later, he passed away following a second cardiac seizure.

Bhag Singh may have gone, but his desk with his notes is intact. To grieve over him or not to grieve over him—that is the question. I suspect he wouldn't have liked that. Because whenever I cried, he was the first to wipe my tears.

The daughter of India's badminton star, Prakash Padukone, slated for a sports career, gravitated towards modelling and the movies. Perfect star material, she debuted in Bollywood with *Om Shanti Om*. Next, she disproved the notion that models can't act, with excellent performances in *Love Aaj Kal, Cocktail* and *Yeh Jawani Hai Deewani,* and is the prime choice for roles which exude glamour as well as dramatic felicity. The tabloid press can't stop tattling about the twists and turns in her private life, which she has handled with in-bred dignity.

DEEPIKA PADUKONE

Sleepless in the moonlight

Thoughts, unending thoughts—bordering on anxiety? 'Girls just wanna have fun' or so they say. There's some of that but plenty of slogging as well, which is why I can't fall asleep—something that's usually as easy as switching off the lights. Guess I am trying to exorcise the day from my system. When one is extremely tired, one can't sleep easily. Never believed that...till today.

Ten hours at the studio, four spent on travelling—I should've been a zombie but my mind's buzzing. Who am I talking to? No one, myself, and everyone. Questions don't need answers.

It's 3 a.m. The sea stretch visible from my room seems to be resting too. Not a ripple, not a wave. The half-moon is shedding a glow. Can't see the stars distinctly, they are just freckles. Not one of those mega-watts moonlit nights which have been the staples of romantic novels. In fact, there is something tender about a night illuminated by a moon, suggesting romance, love, togetherness. But who knows, those picture-book drawings associated with a moon surrounded by stars, as its courtiers, may be a fallacy. A myth? Made-for-each-other—a catchy phrase but sometimes I wonder if there is anything like a perfect pair. Can't be, that's possible only in Robotland. Statistics seem to scream out loud that urban stress, differences are slowly but steadily extinguishing those moonlit nights.

Now, am I being cynical? Looking at the darker side of the moon? Actually, I'm just letting my thoughts run. This new apartment of mine is a sign of my independence. Always wanted to buy and cherish a house of my own. Which girl doesn't? Unless she has this notion that marriage, husband, in-laws, and children are her tradition-mapped destiny. Absolutely natural. No quarrel with that at all. I'd want to be in that situation too but that's still far away. Miles to go before I sleep…with anyone in the same room!

There's something comforting about this house. I can be alone, I need that private space. I haven't recruited any domestic help. Let's see for how long I can zoom up in the elevator, unlock the door, walk in, cook myself a small dinner, go to sleep, like clockwork. Not sure it will last long. I may believe I need solitude but that could be a passing phase. I suspect I need people around me.

The security arrangements at this high-rise seem good but there's always that fear. An intruder? A ghost—ha ha? An extraterrestrial? But then why should any ET alight on my apartment, and not on someone else's. Girl, next you'll be imagining flying saucers descending on the sea right before your eyes. Take light, go to sleep. Pillow, pillow, here I come.

Sorry for the break.

It's 4-ish a.m. Might as well phone a friend. She'll be surprised, happy to hear from me after such a long while. Must be months.

My friend, pick up the phone, pick it up, pick it up. Has she switched off her cell or what? Not fair. Isn't she aware that all of us need a 4 a.m. friend? Or has that species gone extinct?

'Hey, hi!'

'*Aieeeeee*, who's that?'

'Who'd call you at four in the morning?'

'Ohhhh hi. Are you okay? Is everything alright?'

'Yeah, yeah.'

'Then why?'

'Just.'

'Oh...so how's everything going?'

'Good, good, am good. Rocking...I think.'

'You sound strange.'

'Do I? No, no. Just that I haven't spoken to you for long.'

'Yeah...and I've been reading all about your activities in the papers.'

'Don't believe everything you read.'

'I don't but you're having a blast...who would have thought!'

'Stop!'

'Now you've got me wide awake.'

'Sorry, sorry, I'll talk to you at a decent hour.'

'When?'

'Soon.'

'When is sooooon?'

'Come on, it's you who hasn't kept in touch. I'll call whenever you like…tomorrow...now go catch your beauty sleep.'

'Hey, you need to, I don't. *Apun to chakachak hai.*'

'Yeah, yeah, bye.'

'Bye. Don't forget to call.'

'Take care.'

'You too…you need to…ha ha.'

'Ha ha, bye.'

'Bye.'

My best friend too, sigh. She believes in the gossip stuff too. Guess it's human. Still, I think she should know me better. Of course she does, she was just pulling my leg. She shouldn't, she could've at least asked me about my day, how it's gone. Would've given her an update. Would've told her about the interview I did in the afternoon with this senior journalist. Thank god it didn't get gossipy but I wonder what he'll make of it…it went all over the place. Talked for an hour, maybe more. He was taking notes diligently but how on earth will he make sense of those squiggles and wiggles? Must be shorthand, must have learnt it. Whatever, yeah, maybe the interview's got my head buzzing tonight. I'm in replay mode. Now let me remember what I told him. Hope he gets it alright…hope so.

He wanted to know about love, yesterday and today. No clue how he'll make that interesting because my take is nothing spectacular. Told him my idea of romance was formed after watching films like *Dil, Jo Jeeta Wohi Sikandar,*

Baazigar, all seen on video cassettes at home in Bangalore, oops, I mean Bengaluru.

Next, journalist*ji* wanted to know the address in Bengalaru, my birth date and more details which he could have easily Googled but I didn't want to be rude. Rattled them off politely—I was born in Copenhagen where my dad, Prakash Padukone, had gone for training. Eventually, we settled in a three-bedroom apartment on Bengaluru's Cunningham Road. Told him that my dad was on the jury of *Filmfare* awards once, and that there was this big carton of tapes of *Gumrah, Damini, Hum Hain Rahi Pyaar Ke* in the house. Since Dad is a very correct sort of person, he wouldn't allow us to watch the films with him, or influence him in the grading. We were permitted to see only the ones which he recommended, that too when he was out of the house.

I'd whistle when Dad and Mum left home for work. They're such a good-looking couple, the two daughters aren't a patch on Mr Prakash and Mrs Ujjala Padukone. I'd whistle only after they were out of earshot. I was a propah Chitrapur Saraswat Brahmin girl studying at the Sophia High School. Wolf whistles were out of question.

I did start off by saying that perfection is impossible. This may be subjective but I would make an exception in the case of my parents. I love their love story.

Dad was the national badminton champion, he had an aura about him. Mum had her own identity, she works in the travel business. They first noticed each other at the wedding of Mum's elder sister. They were very distantly related. It was love at first sight, wow. Engagement, a wedding, a reception, and then, ahem, I was born. Four years later, Anisha arrived. She's a well-known golfer.

Journalist*ji* nodded. Didn't squiggle all this information. He had done his homework, after all.

Suddenly, the phone shrilled. Hang on…

'Are you sure you're okay? Okay as in really *okay*.'

'Yes, yes. Why aren't you asleep?'

'I was. You woke me up silly. Remember?'

'Oh sorry.'

'Remember to call tomorrow.'

'Yes, of course.'

'You know what! I think something's bothering you.'

'Ohhhho, no. It's just that I was feeling wide awake.'

'You and awake? Lady Kumbhkarna? How did that happen?'

'It's a first.'

'Make it the last. Count sheep.'

'Good idea, I'll try that. Now bye…'

So where was I? 'It's a first,' I'd said. A first at writing too. Let's see how long I can keep this going? The moon, the elusive stars, a pen and paper, perfect! That word's bothering me. Can anything or anyone be *perfect*? Really? As in *really*?

Wish I could short-hand. Just let the thoughts flow for whatever they are worth. So I told journalist*ji*, who was managing the feat of balancing a cup of coffee in one hand and squiggling with the other. On the sofa in a common friend's house. She had vanished. I wish she hadn't. I don't know what

I was saying but journalist*ji* was absorbing it all like a sponge, or pretending to. I'll know what emerges only when I see the piece in print.

Yes, so back to Dad, he was the super sportsman, also worked in an office. Mum, equally focused on her job, continues to be a neatnik, a perfectionist. I suspect I get those traits from her. Dad and Mum are so sweetly conservative. They've completed their 30th wedding anniversary but in all my 26 years, I've never seen them hug each other. If they argue, it's over petty things like Dad leaving his plate at the breakfast table. Mum speaks her mind out, Dad is quiet and reclusive. Opposites who live on the same page.

Mum took leave when I was nervous before the 10th standard Board examinations. And to date, since the last four years that I've been in show business, Dad has never questioned me about the gossip he may have read about me. He's accustomed to such kite-flying, being a sports star himself.

Journalist*ji* asked for a second cup of coffee as I continued to answer his questions on love, yesterday and today. Not that I'm an authority on the subject. But I think I spoke honestly, though I did not see any expression, positive or negative, on his face. He was totally inscrutable, even when we came to the U-turns—as he described them—of love today. Now how did I hold forth on that? I said things to the effect that today's young generation is practical. Tolerance levels are drastically low. Ditto for attention spans. We do give up easily, bin relationships instead of repairing them. We look at our differences, not our similarities.

Naturally, I expressed my dream wish. 'What I want is the harmony I've seen in my parents. I don't have a clue how to go about locating that. All I know is that I can't be calculatingly practical in achieving any goal. Surely I can be a little bit or a lot stupid in love. It's my life. Right?'

'What does love mean to you?' Journalist*ji*'s question was predictable but apt. To which my response was, 'It means losing your emotions. Easier said than achieved, especially in my case, or in the case of most actresses. I have to be away for long spells, weeks and months, shooting abroad. I can't meet someone I love every day. I don't get possessive but yes, there's this aching feeling of missing that person. And it gives rise to the doubt—can love be permanent?'

Journalist*ji* almost spilled his coffee—a reaction at long last!—as I continued on the lines of, 'And so when I've fallen in love, I've been consumed by it. I've been into it with all my heart. And I would say that there can be absolutely sensible reasons for falling out of love. Like maybe two people are just not meant to be with each other.' Then I went on, 'I've learnt a lot about myself in the last four years. I've come closer to myself. See, I can live alone in my apartment, where I can clock in and clock out whenever I want. I've matured. I'm independent, I know what heartache is, I've recuperated and recovered. Today I'm headstrong but not self-indulgent. I can be tough on myself.'

Journalist*ji*'s face remained expressionless. Next, he asked what I expect from a relationship—from love?

'Obviously, I long for the kind of love that has sustained itself between my parents.' I even said, quite strongly, 'For that, it has to be smooth-going from the outset. If the road is rocky from the starting-point of the journey, there will be danger ahead. The man I love should be aware that, together, we can take on the most perilous twists and turns of a highway, shouldn't he?'

Interview over.

From my window, there's no sign of daybreak yet. The half-moon's still on. Wish it would leave politely the way journalist*ji* did. Stop it, stop the day from replaying on the turntable of your mind. Go on, count those sheep, try to snatch some sleep. Should I put on some music? Should have thought of that earlier.

Music! I've been avoiding talking about music. I might as well confess that's what's keeping me awake. I was sure romance, in the traditional sense of the word, was dead. But then last night, I got this text message from someone I had considered very special in my life. Our friendship had disintegrated, and that too somewhat acrimoniously. Last night, this friend sms'ed me, must have been around 10 or 10.30 at night. I thought he was being cute. Cute and smart. The sms message asked, with a smiley, if I nursed any secret desires. Typical of him to use such a word. Desire! Without thinking, I messaged back, 'Yes. Desire to learn to play a musical instrument.'

Within a few hours, must have been a little past midnight, a grand old master piano was delivered to my doorstep.

I've been trying to ignore it...in vain. It's sitting there, right there, right now, bathed in moonlight. There...I have said it. Now you know why I can't sleep. I feel lovely, happy... er...desired.

Love knows no yesterdays or todays. It just is. Perfect...or almost there.

Feisty and indefatigable, she has worn quite a few chapeaux: A-list choreographer, A-list director of *Main Hoon Na* and *Om Shanti Om*, reality show juror and actress. Daughter of Kamran, who hammered out B-grade stunt films in the 1950s, she is mother to triplets, and threatens to author a handbook on raising children.

FARAH KHAN

Guess who came to dinner

Grandma was sporty, not literally, but in the type of visuals she would set off by doing her own interrupted number. So in my eyes and, at times, in imagination, she was this basketball of fire, a cricket ball of googlies, a football of a thousand goals, a ping pong ball of love-all. She was a ball. Not that she was the size and shape of any ball. She was just having a ball with life, and we were standby players on her team. From the benches of her mental stadium, we watched her bend and break every rule of every game. We'd shudder, 'What will she do next?' Maybe pickle us in a jar and serve us for breakfast to the poor.

Now everyone adores their grandmothers. So did we, with all her mega-eccentricities. Other grannies are cuter than buttons. So what? Ours was way superior, more adventurous than Indiana Jones. She wasn't crazy, but she would drive us around the bend. We were sure we'd go down a deep cliff with her, screaming, 'Grrrrrannnnny, we don't want to die. Not so soon.' And this fear of flying down a cliff and becoming a smash-up of bones coursed deep through the veins of my brother Sajid and I. Whenever we saw her, we'd hide behind a tree, a wall, anywhere, holding our breaths, exhaling, but only to hiss, 'Shhhhhhh!' Grandma Perrin was as predatory as a lioness on the loose in the Mumbai jungle, always on the prowl, her age somewhere between seventy-five and eighty be damned. Sajid and I loved her to death, but were afraid—touch this livewire and we'd perish of immediate electric shock.

I must have been thirteen and my brother, eight, when she brought 'Jesus Christ' home. She had this vision that she would serve the Lord, look after him and receive benediction. It was about to be realised. Only she was the sort to mix up the Lord with a hippie, one of the many from the globe wanderers, who must have presumably spent time all over Mumbai's roads, beaches and sleazy lodges. She just had to sight a hippie in a *kurta,* flowing hair and a flowing beard, and that was it. She had to save him from undernourishment. She had to converse philosophically with him, learn of matters which were divine, earn brownie points to reserve her suite in the Buckingham Palace of heaven.

Grandma liked to live in 3-D, although my branch of the family was creaking precariously in a ramshackle building of no dimension, off Juhu beach. Hers, and by default, our lives would change for the better if we were kind to this guest plonked before us. Kindness was expected: offer the guest a meal, a mat to sleep on for the night, and do call for decent cigarettes for him to smoke instead of the smelly joints he was more than likely to pull out of his mirror-work sling bag, this very minute.

Grandma Perrin Irani believed in the healing power of love and faith. She had to, or else she wouldn't have been alive to tell her tale. Born and raised in Nasrabad, if she could be raised, that is, I am sure she grew like a beanstalk on her own fierce terms and conditions. By the way, Nasrabad is a township in Isfahan province in Iran. Even as recently as six to seven years ago, it was home to just 5,750 people from 1,360 families. I suspect she must have been bored, suffocated or terminally restless. Her husband, Nosher in tow, she had arrived in the late 1930s on a storm-tossed steamer to Bombay, where she knocked out a hat-trick of three daughters at swift record-breaking intervals. Her husband couldn't match her lust for life and survival, he retreated into the wings. She was the boss. Possessing the voice of an opera diva, she made it clear to leading film studio owners and producers that her daughters would become celebrities at the movies. They would bring the bread, butter and marmalade home. She would be independent of male support. Preternaturally, Perrin Irani charted the careers for her daughters Daisy and Honey as the most successful kid stars Indian show business has ever known. Iconic, if you ask me.

From the moment Daisy and Honey Aunties could lisp and toddle, they were moppet stars. As for her third daughter, Menka—our mother—she escaped the film studio prisons. No, she wouldn't act, never, never, never, except as an adult heroine some day. More resistant than her sisters, she was sent off to Panchgani to study.

To break away from her mother, Menka eloped with Kamran, a swashbuckling hero-producer-director à la Errol

Flynn, reputed for his action flicks about pirates and rural messiahs, set on land and the high seas, respectively. Yeah, really, it was the other way around. In his films, frequently pirates could land on earth and rural messiahs could be caught on the decks of boats. Why do the predictable? The movies were hits, Kamran was super-dashing, Mum Menka was thoroughly entranced. She acted for her husband, not for her mother. Grandma Perrin pooh-poohed, 'Wait, she will regret all this some day.'

Mum was not affected by the cluck-clucking. But she was certainly affected by Dad Kamran's penchant for women. He brought home another bride, just like that, as if he was bringing home another lamp-shade. Mum walked out on him, moving into a storage room lent to her by one of her sisters. It could barely contain a bed on its last legs, on which Mum, Sajid and I squashed ourselves. In addition, there was a wafer-thin almirah and a micro-table, but no chairs. We ate buffet-style, serving ourselves on tin plates, painting the bedsheet with yellow *daal* dots and squares.

The room smelt permanently of rice, *daal* and kerosene. The stove, which required a muscular amount of pumping, perfumed the room. Mum said the stink was our Chanel No. 5. Mercifully, we were spared the more vicious malodour of the lavatory. It was far from our room. At the overpopulated building's back-end was a common toilet for its residents. We'd run in and out of this stink nightmare in one minute flat, aghast that the obese man next door would be inside for hours, heaven knows doing what! Mum didn't encourage such thoughts. 'Shut up! His wife lets me use her phone sometimes. The man's fat, takes time to load-shed.' Oh. Ok.

Life meant fantasising that our room was as enormous as the whole wide world. Mum didn't ever grumble, neither did Sajid nor I, till Grandma dropped by on a monsoon-ravaged evening, unannounced and unexpected. She had brought along a hippie she had mistaken for an incarnation of Jesus Christ. She spotted him when he was dashing towards a bus-stop for shelter. She was in the midst of her daily evening walk, never mind the weather, when she swooped down upon him. He couldn't be left out in the rain, she brought him under her lady-like umbrella. Catching him by the sleeve, she sprinted across to our house just a hop-skip-and-jump away.

Grandma and my mother Menka hadn't been on talking terms for nearly six months. They had bickered as usual over the Kamran elopement gone wrong. But there she was, Grandma folding up the umbrella, but still drenched from head to toe, accompanied by her wetter hippie.

The man looked at us goofily as if we were monkeys in a zoo. If he had carried peanuts or bananas, he would have surely thrown them at us. What's more, we would have grabbed them. We were hungry. In fact, that evening was special, vis-à-vis the dinner. Daisy Aunty, knowing her sister's taste for fish, had sent over three portions of pomfret fry, marinated with red chillies and turmeric powder. It was an event. The customary *daal-chaawal* with the bonus of fish—food for the gods!

Dinner was just about to be heated on the stove when Grandma and her Hippie Lord took over.

'Feed him! Give him a towel to dry, and some fresh clothes. Let him sleep here tonight,' Grandma ordered imperiously, and promised, 'I will fetch him tomorrow.'

'But...,' Mum interceded weakly.

'No ifs and buts,' she would not discuss the guest and our hosting abilities. 'That's your problem, Menka. You're always going, but, but, but... If you had listened to your mother, you'd be in a grand mansion, not here!'

'Listen...'

'No listening. I'm your mother. If it weren't for me, you wouldn't be on this earth. And see what an opportunity I'm giving you...I have brought Jesus home. Be good to him and your *naseeb* will improve.'

'What?' This couldn't be real. 'I can't afford to feed another mouth. Nothing doing,' Mum was adamant.

'We shall see about that.' The combat continued. 'I'm going now. I have to change or I'll catch a cold...and heyyyy, you two!'

Sajid and I went numb behind the almirah.

Grandma marched up to us and trilled, 'So sweet. See, both of you have inherited my looks.'

We weren't sure whether that was a good thing or a bad thing, but gaped on as she delivered her final command of the evening, 'Your mother doesn't have manners. I hope you two are not like her. Now, you...,' she pointed a finger at Sajid, 'Go, get me a taxi.'

Mum understood she was fighting a losing battle. She said with authority, 'Leave my kids out of this. I'll find you a taxi... sooner the better.'

Grandma had scored another goal: willy-nilly we would have to look after her Lord. Something told me that the dinner we were salivating about, was ruined. The guest would get the pomfret.

Left alone with us, the hippie drawled, 'Hiya kids, how're you doing? I'm Dave from Connecticut. Heard of it?'

We didn't bat an eyelid. He could have been from Mars for all we cared.

Hippie Lord elaborated, 'Guys, don't worry. I don't bite.' Comforting us, the wet guest sat down on the floor, pulled out a rosary bead and went into deep prayers. His language we couldn't decipher. It could have been a *shloka* or a hymn.

Mum returned, looking as martyred as Joan of Arc. There was nothing she could do. She served two portions of the fish for Sajid and me, sacrificing her protein rush for the guest. He was given a napkin (no towels) and a change of clothes. Naturally, this twenty-fiveish-year-old Lord couldn't fit into Sajid's pyjamas or trousers.

Mum quizzed him seriously, 'Do you mind wearing my clothes for the night?'

He didn't. Dinner completed in fast motion, Dave accepted the clothes as if they were frankincense and myrrh. He returned from the lavatory without a change of facial or any other expression. Next, he curled up on the *chatai* and used a stack of newspapers for a pillow. That was Mum's ingenuous idea. Actually he looked quite angelic in Mum's white petticoat and red blouse. When Sajid and I giggled, he was pleased, 'These are very comfortable. Thank you...and good night.' He rolled over to one side and was soon fast asleep.

Mum wouldn't switch off the lights. She said she wasn't about to sleep with a stranger in a dark room.

'Why?' Sajid probed.

'Never mind,' Mum said wearily. 'You're too small to understand.'

But I wasn't. Obviously Mum had her apprehensions: what if he was an avatar not of Jesus, but of Raman Raghav or Jack the Ripper?

The night passed by uneventfully, but Mum was seething. As soon as it was daybreak, she rushed to the neighbours to use their phone.

Daisy Aunty couldn't believe her ears. Honey Aunty believed her ears and said, 'What's new? You know it could be worse.' The sisters' phone conference led to the decision: wait for Mum to retrieve her property. If Grandma didn't take the guest back as she had promised, 'something' would have to be done.

'Why don't you give this guy shelter...and food? We don't have much!' Mum kept arguing.

The sisters pointed out that they had husbands and kids to look after. They couldn't welcome a hippie home, their husbands would be enraged. Mum was placated: be patient, their mother may be many things, but she always kept her word.

'Let's see,' Mum, the tragedy queen, gave up. 'If she doesn't...'

'What will you do then?' Daisy Aunty rolled her tongue in cheek. 'Call the municipality van to pick up garbage. You know you can't throw him out. Can you?'

'I can, but I'm a bit scared...'

'Now what? Why?'

'Our great mamma has said that he may be a reïncarnation of Jesus Christ...what if she's right? I'll be in trouble.'

'Menka, you are as nuts as she is.'

Mum agreed, 'Can't help it. I have her blood inside me.'

'Then suffer. And wait till she returns.'

'And if she doesn't?'

Daisy Aunty must have banged down the phone.

Mum now looked reverentially at the guest. Still wearing a petticoat and blouse, Dave made himself absolutely at home. And afraid that lightning may strike her, Mum dipped into her tiny savings, to boil him two eggs for breakfast, and for lunch, lamb stew along with the must-devour *daal* and *chaawal*.

Around tea-time, Mum was nervous. She couldn't contact the Lord's benefactor, no one was picking up Grandma's phone. Daisy and Honey Aunties felt she would come to claim her property, sooner or later. 'And look,' Honey Aunty pointed out, 'this guest of yours must have special powers. It has stopped raining today.'

'Oh, that it has...do you really think Lord Issu has something to do with it?'

'Yes, of course.'

Mum served the hippie high tea, *bhajias*, and chocolate-cream biscuits borrowed from the neighbours. And by evening, 7.30 p.m. or so, the rains returned. This was getting very baffling. Can this guest control the monsoon or not? We never found out.

Grandma Perrin arrived at long last, at 8 p.m., saving Mum the onus of rustling up dinner for the guest. She took one look at the cross-dressed Dave, and to our surprise, complimented him, 'The clothes suit you...now come, let's go.' And off they went, our room restored to its original Atlas-sized world.

Curiously, all of us in that room were sad to see the overnight guest leave. For Sajid and me, that meant, no side-dishes during a meal. For Mum, his departure meant the lingering doubt...what if he truly was...? We didn't help Mum with filling in the blank. We didn't know either.

Grandma disappeared with her Lord Issu. Her home was padlocked. The three sisters weren't worried, she'd be fine whether she was in the company of a don, or Dracula. She was quite capable of pulling a trigger at a don and extracting a vampire's tooth. But her 'Hello, how are you?' gang of friends missed her, and would inquire when she would be back on her evening walks from Khar to Bandra Bandstand, and occasionally to Juhu beach. Her friends, none of whom was ever invited over to her house in Khar—she liked to maintain a distance—had nicknamed her Indira Gandhi behind her back. A bit inaccurate that. Grandma had this black streak running through her white hair, while Indira Gandhi's style was a white streak in grey-black hair. And she wore a *jhaba,* Grandma that is, a loose flowing gown, close to the Arabic *djelleba,* but not quite.

Unexpectedly, Grandma renewed regular contact with her prodigal daughter Menka. She would call at the neighbour's to report about her travels with Lord Issu. Initially, she had shown him around Mumbai. They had watched all the movies there were to watch. Then they had hung out for a fortnight gazing at the clouds over the ghats of Lonavla-Khandala. Not enough. Grandma and her companion travelled for months, completing an India darshan of sorts. For a long time, they combed the beaches of Goa. And her conviction strengthened that he was a visitor from another time and space. How come? It seems there was power failure throughout Goa when they arrived there on bus. As soon as they reached the hotel, abracadabra, all the lights came on. The air-conditioners too.

'Now is that a sign or is it not?' Grandma asked of Mum who was actually bewitched by the information, and quite pleased with the announcement that they would be returning to Bombay within a couple of days. Much against her will, Mum found herself pleading, 'Oh, I do hope he will stay with us again.'

'No, no,' came Grandma's answer. 'He'll be staying in a good hotel.'

'You have so many rooms,' Mum jogged her memory. 'He can stay with you, can't he?'

'Stupid, he likes luxuries and room service.'

'Oh, does he?'

'Yes, we must do all we can to make him feel that we, his subjects, are kind and considerate. There will be no Judas in our midst.'

'Mummy, but do you have that kind of money to blow up? You're not putting him up in a five-star, are you?'

'Hush, Menka. What is money?'

'Then…'

'Then what? I've sold all my jewellery.'

'Mummmmm! You didn't.'

'Don't tell me you expected to inherit anything from me. Not a single paisa I will give to you girls.'

'To your grandchildren?'

'Of course, I will give them...'

'What? Your flat at least...'

'That I will be selling off as soon as I return...'

'Nooooo!'

'I will give them my love and memories.'

Now the three sisters were horrified in equal measure. Their mother was totally unilateral and impulsive. It was important to be very careful. They had to be sensitive even if she wasn't. And Grandma Perrin had her wonderful qualities too. Faith was her only motivation; transiently she had believed in every faith. She was a pukka Zoroastrian, visiting the agiary every week. Then she claimed that a *pir* had appeared in her dreams. The religious leader, whom she had never met, made such a strong impression in her dream that she converted to Islam for two to three years. Then she saw Shivji in her dreams and would pray at temples. Next, she took the tenets of Christianity very seriously. That was the time she had picked up Dave from the bus-stop.

No one, leave alone her daughters, could question her self-piloted voyage into secularism. But she had to be controlled, she was getting on in years. The sisters weren't sure if she was in her senses.

At that advanced age, Grandma didn't need a pair of spectacles, despite her hobby of doing needlepoint embroidered portraits. She'd be at work as soon as a new President of the US was elected. President Jimmy Carter was the only one who acknowledged her gift with a handwritten letter to express his thanks.

Needlepoint embroidery had now been replaced by a state of mind—that she had indeed rescued her Lord from rain and starvation. Alarming, alarming, alarming, the sisters couldn't take her indulgences any more. Daisy Aunty took the lead, she would handle the situation surely, but delicately.

Grandma arrived with her travelling companion. Sajid and I couldn't recognise him. He wasn't wearing a petticoat and blouse, he was in designer jeans and a Polo T-shirt. His dirty blonde hair no longer fell over his forehead, he had got himself a buzz cut. Add to that Nike shoes, spiffy glass frames highlighting his blue eyes, and a Cartier watch. He looked like Robert Redford.

Daisy Aunty called him at the swanky hotel where he was staying, and invited herself to tea. It was at her mother's expense anyway. At the café, she didn't waste much time on ceremony. 'Mister, get the hell out of my mother's life. How long is your visa for, anyway?' she narrowed her eyes and delivered the punch-line, 'Meet her again and I'll get the police here.'

Lord Dave was so taken aback that he didn't finish his coffee and croissant. He vanished with his Burberry bags, never to be seen again.

Grandma Perrin wasn't distraught or heartbroken. She surmised that he must have had to take off for several other divine appointments, but she did say, 'I wish he had called before leaving...or at least left a note.'

Daisy Aunty took care of that. She wrote one in big block letters so that her handwriting wouldn't be recognised. The Lord had instructed Grandma to 'SERVE HUMANITY AND FULFILL ALL YOUR RESPONSIBILITIES TOWARDS YOUR DAUGHTERS. TAKE CARE OF THEM. YOU TAKE CARE TOO. AMEN.'

Grandma Perrin mellowed. For ten years after Lord Issu's departure, she behaved like a lamb. She always kept rosary beads, a *rudraksha mala* and a *taweez* by her side. In the mid-1990s, she suffered a major stroke and lay in a coma for nearly a week at the Holy Family Hospital.

One day, she woke up, bright and cheerful. The doctors and nurses rushed to her. She looked at them, knew where she was and why, and then asked the senior doctor, 'Can you get me a Mangola, fast?'

The doctor wasn't sure whether he should. She grabbed hold of his hand, asked for the drink again, specifying that it should be chilled. Mangola was brought to her, she gulped it down gratefully, said, 'Bye' and passed away, taking the first step on the stairway to heaven.

She had done so much to book her passage there.

The former Miss India became the darling of the nation when she was introduced in the Romeo-and-Julietesque *Qayamat se Qayamat Tak*. Associated with light-hearted roles, she affirmed her gift for comedy with *Hum Hain Raahi Pyaar Ke*, and featured with every frontline hero in gamine, romantic roles. Associated with a clean-cut image, she models, and acts occasionally in film roles of spleen and substance. Prime examples: *My Brother Nikhil*, *I Am* and *Gulabi Gang*. Among her hidden skills are proficiency at classical singing.

JUHI CHAWLA

Almost a fairy tale till...

A light mist rises, stars sparkle, the leather-bound cover opens up to the first chapter of a fairy tale, which invariably establishes a beautiful, faraway world. Unless it's about dear Cinderella, who found happiness only towards the closing pages. There's Red Riding Hood, too, who was almost gobbled up by the big bad wolf. There are exceptions to the rule.

My fairy tale fell into the wondrous realm. So there I was this happy child, reaching Fort Convent, by car or the school bus. Our home—a cosy apartment in Cuffe Parade—was inhabited by Mona my mother, Desraj my father, Aunt Veena, my brother and I. Bobby, my brother, was always up to pranks. I was the good girl, sugar and spice, and everything nice. Warring siblings—every home should have a pair who are into petty arguments. Prepares them for the bigger ones to be tackled in life, with others. If the house was bedecked with balloons and buntings on my birthday, he'd want to tear them down till I screamed, 'Do that and I'll kill you!'

At school, I would sit primly, figuring out geometry and logarithms. Numbers were confusing. At times, I wondered why Dad and Mom were arguing. He was an income tax officer and Mom worked in the hotel industry. Dad doted on me. Unfairly, I doted on Mom. She would monitor that homework done, it was early to bed, and early to rise for her princess. Not a pretty princess exactly. I wasn't peaches-and-cream. Had this light wheatish complexion of a Punjabi girl.

Every girl hoped to be noticed by the boys from the nearby Campion School. Strangely enough, I was, but couldn't tell Mom, Dad or Bobby that. For all his bullying ways, Bobby was so possessive that he would have slaughtered any boy who dared to cast a second look at his kid sister. The Chawla family was like that, bickering at home, but morphing into each other's protective lieutenants outside. It was all about adoring the family.

Kathak classes, diction coaching from the sprightly Pearl Padamsee for whom phonetics was as natural as breathing, were a part of growing up. That I would become a movie star some day wasn't even a pipe dream. No one harboured that ambition for me. No one considered me attractive till I was in the tenth standard. I had gone over to the Taj Mahal Hotel on my way home from school to pick up Mom. She happened to be supervising some work in the health club. Mumtaz, the epitome of glamour, took one look at me, and told Mom, 'You have a very pretty daughter.' I was flying.

At HR College, I became self-conscious. The plain duckling was swanning. Suddenly, I was being noticed by the boys. Sumeet looked at me as if I had stepped down from heaven. That became a turning point. It does for so many girls. It happened to Cinderella. What if she hadn't sneaked into the grand ball and left her slipper behind for Prince Charming?

Sumeet's sister, Sangeeta Chopra, was organising a fashion show in New Delhi. When a model didn't show up, I was asked if I'd be the substitute. 'Sure,' I drawled. 'No problems,' though I was shivering like a wet mouse within. Backstage, it was chaos. Models were crying. Some accessories hadn't arrived. It was nerve-rattling. I survived. Then a girl from college was entering the Miss India contest. That was the topic of the month in the college canteen. A friend of mine said, 'If she can, why can't you?' My clothes were borrowed, my make-up was slapped on any which way. This time I wasn't shivering. My teeth were rattling with fright that evening at the Shanmukhanada Hall. I smiled, I must have said all the right things. The beauty pageant was sponsored by Kaysons, a sari brand. The final question I had to answer was about what's common between the sari brand and life. Smartly, I said, 'Both come in all colours.' Applause and huh?, I was crowned Miss India...by Rekhaji. Yaaaaay!

Almost every actor, I believe, loves his or her childhood, and banks overwhelmingly on the emotions experienced in the course of coming of age. There is a tendency to erase the unpleasant, and to encash the pleasant from the ATM of the mind. I can think this way now—of the glorious girly years and of the god-granted opportunities.

Khayyam, the veteran music composer, was a friend of the family. He told Mom categorically that the film industry was no place for her daughter to be in. Mom would have liked me to move on to study for an MBA degree. I wouldn't, or couldn't even think of it. There was that swirl of potential stardom around me.

There were mistakes, self-centredness. I can no longer conceal them. My story would lack honesty if I didn't admit that after *Qayamat Se Qayamat Tak, Bol Radha Bol, Raju Ban Gaya Gentleman* and *Hum Hain Raahi Pyaar Ke,* I felt I was happening. Dad doted on me even more than he did before. Mom was happy, but she knew that stardom is transient. It could peak, it could crash. But somewhere down the line, I cared only for those things which mattered to me immediately. My career, my popularity, were all I could see, my vision blinkered. It was me-me-me. The mirror and the inquiring gaze of the camera didn't unnerve me anymore.

Mom gifted me a pair of solitaire diamond ear-rings. Parents are taken for granted, aren't they? I gave her nothing. I never lavished on her the love she deserved.

Mom should have been the star, not me. The daughter of a barrister, she was a strikingly tall and handsome woman. Her photos had been sent to BR Chopra for a role in one of his films. I presume she wasn't selected. Coincidentally, neither was I when my photos were sent to him for the role of Draupadi in the TV series 'Mahabharata'. Unlike me, she didn't ever think of acting again.

For her, it had been an arranged marriage to Desraj Chawla, who had joined the income tax cadre after sitting for the IAS examinations. I'm told that Mom was drawn towards an army officer—men in uniform do exude a distinct charisma. But she didn't let anyone, even the army officer get a hint about that. She agreed to marry the gentle and soft-spoken income tax officer as soon as they met at a family gathering in New Delhi. Arranged marriages were the norm, she had no objections to that. Dad was genial, it seemed as if they were meant for each other. They would love vacationing in Mussoorie and Shimla.

Dad would read out 'Ripley's Believe It or Not' column to his children on Sunday mornings. One of Dad's favourite sayings was, 'To build a bridge, first find a river.' I'd done both. A streak of arrogance was mounting and I wasn't even aware of it. I was working round the clock, trying to do my best—snag all the A-list projects and A-grade awards.

How it all comes back to me today. I loved Mom, but I wasn't treating her right, perhaps unknowingly, perhaps carelessly. Inexcusable. We were travelling by bus in Switzerland, on the way to the location for *Darr*. I was a star. Mom was sitting behind with the assistant cameramen. I was getting irritated. Why should the heroine's mother be sitting with anyone else, but with the heroine? Didn't Mom know she was a star's mom? I wanted her to change her seat right away. I raised my voice very rudely on her. A little later, Shah Rukh Khan chastised me, 'Don't ever do that! Parents go away before you do...and you won't be able to turn back the clock. You'll live with regrets.'

That was the first wake-up call, but my eyes were still closed to Mom's feelings. A year-and-a-half later, we were shooting for *Duplicate*. At the unit's hotel in Prague, Mom was reading

Anna Karenina by the bedside lamp. I had been told by the unit that she had forgotten to get the keys to our baggage. The locks had to be broken. I screamed at her, 'I have to get up at five in the morning for the rehearsals and all you can do is read!'

During the night, I could hear her shuffling. I could sleep only fitfully. When it was time for me to leave, she was still reading.

The last time I saw her, she was tying the laces of her walking shoes. I returned in the evening to find the room exactly the way I had left it. I had thrown a tantrum, walked off like a hurricane. She hadn't picked up any of the clothes strewn around the room. And *Anna Karenina* was on the bedside table...open at the page she had last read. She hadn't returned.

'Has anyone seen Mom?' I ran around, asking everyone in the hotel. No answer, it was scary.

She was gone, in a road accident.

I'd done her wrong. I hadn't appreciated her when she was there. I can never atone for that.

And to think I loved my mother so intensely that when I was a child, I'd get these recurring dreams that something terrible was happening to her. Like she was engulfed by fire or had fallen down a very steep staircase. She was asthmatic. One night, during a particularly bad attack, I had clung on to her, crying out loud, 'Mom, don't leave me...please don't.'

In Prague, she did leave, walking away never to return. A couple of years later, Dad passed away, and then my aunt. My brother suffered a stroke following a burst aneurism, and has been lying in a coma at a hospital. There's no one around to bully me anymore. No one reading by the bedside lamp anymore. No more 'Ripley's Believe It or Not'.

My life is yoked to my husband and two children. I have not been alone. That can be the only explanation why I could come to terms with the quick succession of tragedies in my family. I kept myself together, I think, also by extending myself as an actress. Onir's *My Brother Nikhil* was the kind of cause-driven cinema which I was unfamiliar with. I was not sure about fitting in. It was a penniless unit. I had to get my costumes, work on my make-up on my own. Usually there's an entire battery of specialists to look after such aspects.

In the film, there's a scene in which I refuse to go and see my brother who's dying of AIDS. It was to happen, in a different way, when my brother went into a coma. I have had the courage to face facts today to a degree because I went through this already in *My Brother Nikhil*.

Years after it was made, it's still invited for viewing the world over. It was being screened at a festival in Germany. I was sitting in the foyer when a woman came up and said that Bobby had helped her in researching a book. She asked me how he was and gave me a copy of the book. At that moment, I went inside the auditorium right into the scene which depicts my inability to face my brother lying in hospital.

What else can I say, but that I broke down? The film resides within me. That scene which I was watching again after a break of seven years, and what I was going through personally, were identical. That evening at the festival, I said to myself, 'I don't want to be brave anymore. I don't need to go into that zone at all. Handle life the way it wants you to. You're not at the centre of things.'

My story is back to the same dot. It started off as a fairy tale. Then reality seeped in. Stories don't always have a happy ending...far from it. Which is why today, a voice within me laughs, 'Girl, you're grown up. You're no longer stupid and innocent.'

That awareness is the only gift I can give to Mom...but much too little and too late.

Witty and wise way beyond his years when he directed his first feature film *Kuch Kuch Hota Hai* at the age of 25, he has confected affection-sprinkled romances and family stories, opting for a twist of sobriety with *My Name is Khan*. A charismatic TV host, and a prolific film producer, he has steadily but surely elevated Dharma Productions into a mega-major force in showbiz. His father, the widely-admired Yash Johar, paved the way for KJo's triumphs.

KARAN JOHAR

Speaking of Mr and Mrs Pinto

They were cool, yet quaint. The bougainvillea-shaded verandah of their wooden-beamed apartment in Colaba overlooked a small handkerchief garden, and a swing which no one ever used.

Every weekend afternoon, a curfew-like silence took over the bylane of Colaba where Mr and Mrs Pinto had lived for as long as they could remember. On these traditional leisure days, the Pintos, like their neighbours, would be lost to the world between 2 p.m. and 4 p.m. After that, a batch of students would troop up the staircase to learn how to stand, engineer their hand movements and, above all, speak with the strength of Brutus at Julius Caesar's funeral.

Mr Daniel Pinto was Mumbai's sole authority on the fine art of public speaking. Tanned, clean-shaven, smart, he changed his suit—in shades of indigo, grey and navy blue—every day of the week. His trousers, a white shirt tucked in, were held up by red suspenders. His Oxford tie would sport a crisp *samosa*-shaped knot, and at times he'd wear a bow-tie which gave him a jauntier demeanour. His shoes shone and twinkled, thanks to regular applications of Cherry Blossom boot polish.

Mrs Margaret Pinto, slightly taller than his 5′ 6″ frame, wore her hair in a bouffant which had stopped halfway under construction. She would get the greying hair lacquered at the beauty parlour down the road, and wore Egyptian cotton skirts with knitted tops in shades of brown. Over the weekends, she was more relaxed, in slacks and white shirts with minimalist embroidery. If she wished to be even more relaxed, she would toss on a *batik kaftan* which swept the floor.

He was lean, she double his size if not more, perhaps due to an inherited metabolism. They would banter about her weight, but never before the students. Professional sangfroid had to be maintained. He threatened to return to Goa some day, she would suggest Pune, 'Dear, that's where everyone is retiring nowadays.' He wanted clarification: what or whom did she mean by 'everyone'? And she would shush him up with one of those withering looks as if to say, 'Danny, you know what I mean.' Future plans would end with the acknowledgement, 'Yes Maggie, I know what you mean. But we do have to plan our retirement, sooner or later.'

Every syllable and consonant was pronounced to perfection. He was Prof Higgins to an equally articulate Mrs Higgins. Mr Pinto's accent was more British than the *London Times*. The origin of his accent, and his education were never questioned. That would have been blasphemous. The man was just born literate and suave: a gentleman and a teacher.

Mr and Mrs Pinto, in harmony with themselves and with the world, breakfasted at a table with carved wooden legs. Freshly-squeezed *mosambi* juice, cereals, half-boiled eggs and Nilgiri tea were their morning pick-me-ups. Grace would be said at every meal. And Teddy, their ageing Labrador, would wait patiently during the thanksgiving prayers before frisking up for his share of toast. Lunch and dinner timings had to be 1 p.m. and 8 p.m. Around Christmas, a thimbleful of sherry for Mrs Pinto and a couple of Scotches for Mr Pinto were mandatory. Once a month at least, Mr and Mrs Pinto would be seen, arm-in-arm, at an opera performance, a Western classical music concert, or the opening of an exhibition at the JJ Art Gallery.

Their house was open on weekends only to a select batch of students who were interviewed and granted the privilege of 'special attention', conditional to their sincerity and desperation to learn. During the week, Mr Pinto would coach students at the Indo-American Society's office at Fort or at the conference rooms let out by the Taj Mahal Hotel. Piano teacher Mrs Pinto had separate days earmarked for separate schools.

It was extremely difficult to get admission to the exclusive weekend classes, consisting of no more than ten students, at the Pintos' Colaba home. And Mr Pinto was a taskmaster, he couldn't be browbeaten either. Discipline was as important as punctuation marks in his book of rules. A story went that in the midst of one of the elite classes at home, a nouveau riche teenager, probably high on marijuana, attempted to get funny, calling his teacher a 'hoax', followed by unmentionable expletives. Mr Pinto glided towards him with a smile, picked him up by the ear, dragged him to the door and said, 'Thank you very much. Your fees will be returned by postal order.' Amiable expression retained throughout, he brushed one hand with the other as if to clean each one of them of dirt, returned to the podium, and said, 'And so where were we?'

To start with, I signed up for thrice-a-week classes conducted at the Indo-American Society's Arctically air-conditioned office at Fort. We were at a long, oval table, thirty or thirty-five of us, an assortment of speech-challenged people. The 'challenged' part varied. Young corporate executives and marketing whiz kids were there to enhance their gift of the gab. A group of housewives had come together to learn the finer points of conversing with their husbands' business clients. A fortyish man from a business family wanted to become more 'stylish.' And there I was, about thirteen or fourteen years old then, wanting, wishing, praying that I could turn into a man. Literally. I was aware that I was effeminate and overweight, traits I would be reminded of every day at school. I was called 'fatty,' 'a pansy', or both. The word 'gay' hadn't come into common usage then.

I wouldn't play gully cricket with the boys, I would prefer playing hopscotch with the girls. I wasn't ever likely to find place among the school's football team. So what? My mother would never find fault with me, showering me with limitless love. My father too was convinced I was flawless. He was an angel from heaven. Dad had married late. I was born to him when he was forty. He was my two-in-one, a dad and granddad.

It would be facile to trace the reason for my effeminacy to the fact that I was over-protected and over-sheltered by my parents. Mum would smart whenever some kids at school made me feel awful, she'd take me in her arms and kiss me silly. The only child, I was cocooned. Joint decision taken, Mum and Dad did try to send me away to boarding school in a bid perhaps to toughen me up. That was a catastrophe. It was a school where many of the students' parents were either dead or divorced. Many of them had seen their parents argue and separate. I had no such issues. If I was brimming over with complexes, it was only about my own shortcomings.

As soon as I reached the school at Panchgani, I wanted to die. I was ragged for two consecutive days in the toilet, I was miserable, I wouldn't eat, or drink water. Tina and Chinke Kapadia were at the same school. Seeing me bawling away, Tina advised me, 'If you're so unhappy, don't take it. It's your life, take charge of it. Run away.'

I did. I had to catch the next bus to Mumbai somehow. Maybe the tuck money I had would buy me a ticket. On the way to the bus-stop in the thick of the night, I ran through the forest, scared, and rolled down a slope. I was bruised all over. Some local people found me and carried me back to the school. Next, I was in the school's infirmary running a high temperature.

Mum was beside herself. Dad was there within a few hours. As soon as I saw him, I wept, 'I miss you Dad, I miss Mum.' It hadn't been the best way to escape the boarding school, but it worked. I was back home. Mum may have been disappointed, but melted. She had studied at a boarding school in Nainital. Surely her son could have accepted and adapted to a life away from home. 'Sorry,' is all I could say. 'Mum, I'm not you.'

That was stating the obvious. Mum lowered her voice to express what had been bothering her, 'I can understand what you're going through. But tell me, do you want to remain mediocre?' I had no answer. I had never won a trophy, medal or even a consolation prize certificate.

At school in Mumbai, close to my home in the high-rise Acropolis on Malabar Hill, I recovered my security blanket. Mum was just a shout away, not that it helped. I continued to be victimised as the girly boy. Providentially, at a stage when I was in senior school, I came across a small ad for Mr Daniel Pinto's public-speaking classes. Surreptitiously, I joined up. I sneaked the money for the fees by lying to my parents. I hate lying, but it had to be done. I said I wanted to join computer classes, the done thing then. Paranoid that they would detect my lie, I would make sure no one knew where I went, flagging down a taxi, looking over my shoulder to see if anyone was watching, and jumping inside to tell the cabby my destination in a hushed whisper. The taxi drivers must have thought I was strange. But then so did everyone I knew.

A couple of weeks later, Mr Pinto asked me to stay back for a minute after class. He inquired with concern, 'Son, is something bothering you? You're such a sweet child, you should be happy and confident.' I nodded uncertainly. 'Tell you what!' he boomed, 'Treat me like family. You could come to the smaller classes at my home from next weekend.

That way, I can give you more attention.' I wasn't sure. Where would I cadge the money for the exclusive coaching? As if he had read my thoughts, he smiled, 'No extra charge! Now come on, give us a smile.'

I had never felt more elated in my life. Someone was treating me with empathy. I wasn't a freak. Someone could detect that I was the way I was, not out of choice, but because I knew no other way to conduct myself. If anyone could sort me out, it was Mr Pinto. Now that I had been accepted in the elite circle of students, it was a quantum leap towards progress.

Needless to say, Mrs Pinto was the priceless bonus at the Colaba home classes. The first weekend, I thought I went by unnoticed. Then to my surprise, she said, 'I've been watching you, boy. Daniel has been speaking about you quite often.'

'I hope he says nice things,' I said shyly.

'Oh yes,' she loomed over me. 'Daniel never has anything bad to say about anyone. But neither does he have nice things to say about anyone.'

I blushed. She handed over an aluminum foil-wrapped packet to me, 'Some apple pie for you. Baked it myself.'

Taken aback, I stared at the packet as if it was a grenade.

'Come on, Karan. It's not poisoned,' she chortled.

'Of course not, Mrs Pinto,' I corrected my look to one of gratitude. 'Thank you so much. I love apple pies, though I shouldn't be eating fattening stuff.'

'Nonsense! You're a growing boy. You'll get rid of your baby fat.'

'Really?'

The packet was now in my hand. At home, I would have to explain where the pie came from and why. I gobbled it down as fast as I could during the taxi ride home. As soon as I entered, Dad asked, 'So how are the computer classes going? Do you want me to get you a computer?'

'No,' I almost yelled.

'Why? You can practise at home instead of disappearing for hours and hours for the classes...'

'Dad! NO! We're told to learn at the class only...'

'Is that a rule out there?'

Before my lie went all over the place, I said, 'Yes. Dad you ask too many questions.'

'I just want to help you, *yaar*.'

'Dad, can I do things my way, if you don't mind?'

'Let him be, and don't call him "*yaar*",' Mum butted in.

Relief.

The Pintos' home was *paradiso*. Mrs Pinto would feed me sandwiches, plum cakes and marzipan, and brew coffee for me after the rest of the students had left. I would be instructed to stay on, but not talk about the post-classes treat with the others. They would feel left out. In any case, I didn't want the students to pick on me for my privileged status with the Pintos. 'Teacher's pet, teacher's pet!' Who needs to hear that!

The public-speaking guru and the piano teacher were so vibrant and colourful, but beneath that veneer, I could detect loneliness and melancholia. To a degree, I was baffled. Why was I chosen to become the special one? Silly question. Obviously, because I needed a makeover much more than the others did.

Besides assuring me that I was normal, Mr Pinto encouraged self-improvement. I would have to overcome my fears and personality disorders on my own. 'You're not being spoon-fed,' he said one day with unexpected rudeness. 'Your hands flop, you have limp wrists, you are effeminate. Accept that and understand that in the real world, you have to be your gender. Grow up! Become a man.'

My eyes were about to get teary. He could see that, but didn't soften his tone. His mantra to me was, 'Make your life in a box. Never leave what you are, contain yourself. Tell yourself that you will excel, never mind the humiliation you have to endure en route. Those who insult you today will eat their words tomorrow.'

To repair my voice, Mrs Pinto pitched in. I had to put on a baritone husk. I wasn't sure how. 'Just go ahead,' she imitated a man's voice. 'Put it on, fake it. Keep trying, it'll become a habit.' This voice alteration, I did by reciting Alfred Noyes' poem *Highway Man* whenever I was sure no one was listening. Once, Mum caught me at it and arched an eyebrow to which I arched mine too, 'It's just for my literature class at school, Mum. A poetry test is coming up. Do you mind?'

'Huh, why should I mind? But would you mind telling me why you are sounding as if you're making a meal out it?'

"Ooof Ma, I have to recite it with the right diction. Wait, now see how this sounds.'

One more lie.

The wind was a torrent of darkness among the gusty trees,
The moon was a ghostly galleon tossed upon cloudy seas,

The road was a ribbon of moonlight over the purple moor,
And the highwayman came riding—
Riding—riding—
The highwayman came riding, up to the old inn-door.

Mum rolled her eyes and left the room before I could approach the next stanza. She sensed that there was something fishy about this poem practice. There must be a reason why I didn't want to tell her. By contrast, the Pintos heard me struggle through the phonetics of the same poem for two years. They never asked me to leave or hint that I was taking an inordinately long time to get my act right. They had stopped accepting a fee from me. Instead, I was their weekend-lunch companion, and a fixture at the Easter and Christmas celebrations. At home and at school, no one noticed that I was undergoing a personality change. My parents must have attributed it to the fact that I was no longer a baby.

When it was time to leave, move on, devote long hours to the college regimen, in parting Mrs Pinto said, 'Great. Now you don't need us. All we ask of you, Karan, is one thing...'

'Sure. Of course,' I responded.

'All we ask of you is to stay in touch. Don't forget your Danny Uncle and Maggie Aunty.'

She clutched me to her heart for a long time. Before Mrs Pinto let go of me, she kissed my cheeks and forehead. Mr Pinto, not as demonstrative, offered me a strong handshake and said with a spring in his voice, 'Boy, I agree with Maggie for once,' and laughed with his patented bonhomie. 'Don't you ever forget us. Keep in touch. We will miss you.'

From the verandah, I saw the swing in the garden. Empty as always. I didn't break into tears. They wouldn't have liked me to—boys…men don't cry—but I cried all the way home during the taxi ride. I knew that I had used them. I hadn't returned the love they had lavished on me unconditionally. I didn't realise it then, but I do now at the age of forty. I was the son they never had, but I couldn't give them that distinctive measure of love, respect and reverence which a son reserves for his real parents. I was a surrogate son to them, but they weren't my surrogate parents. They couldn't be, even if I tried to give them an identical status. Dad and Mum were irreplaceable. The Pintos knew it too, and saw me leave their house, with a simple, 'Keep in touch.'

I plead guilty. I didn't.

Straightened out, I was no longer squeamish about my voice or body language. I relished the equality with others of my age and gender. The Pintos had never asked for my phone number at home. I hadn't given it either, afraid that my parents would discover my double life. Dad did keep wondering why I wasn't enthusiastic about his persistent offers of setting me up with a computer. I didn't have the guts to reveal my two years of secrets and lies.

On an impulse, long after that perfunctory farewell to the Pintos, I called up. Mrs Pinto was on the line. She was glad to hear my baritone voice, and asked about how I was doing at college. I gave her all the excruciating details, and then asked, 'How is Mr Pinto? May I speak to him, please?'

'But he's gone, dear,' she said. Her voice went flat as she ended, 'We all have to go some day. He would have loved to see you, but we didn't want to disturb...'

'May I come over now and see you, Mrs Pinto?'

She paused and then said, 'Of course, any time, my dear. You'd make this old woman happy.'

The Colaba house was bereft of its grand piano. Mrs Pinto, shrunk to half her size, had sold the piano. She didn't want to give lessons any more, she wanted to spend the rest of her days reading and praying, with her niece Myra by her side. Teddy had passed away soon after Mr Pinto. 'Now I am waiting for my turn,' she said, but added, 'come on, give us a smile. All of us—Teddy, Danny and I—have played a good innings.'

Following a massive heart attack, Mr Pinto had died without so much as a warning. He had returned from the classes at the Indo-American Society late one evening when he felt uneasy. In less than an hour, before a doctor could arrive, he was off.

Mrs Pinto did not reveal this to me, but Myra did on our way down the stairs. Her aunt had cancer, she didn't have many days left. It would be nice if I could drop by once in a while.

I lost that opportunity as well to pay my dues to the Pintos. I was leaving for the U K in less than a week.

When I last saw Mrs Pinto, it was with a bunch of dahlias which she asked Myra to arrange in the empty cut-glass vase immediately. And then she smiled broadly, 'This is so sweet of you, my boy. Danny had a thing for red roses, but it's dahlias for me. No one brings flowers here anymore, but...,' and she stopped. Adjusting herself in the armchair, she wished me luck and said what my mother does whenever I'm travelling overseas, '*Bacha*, look after yourself. It gets very cold out there. Always keep warm.'

And her last sentence to me was, 'Do keep in touch.'

Again, I couldn't. When I called a few weeks later from the UK, Myra announced, 'She's gone.'

But not without making me a man. The Pintos gave me the gift of realising my small and big dreams—of compering film award shows, talking tall from public platforms, hosting TV shows and judging reality shows. So whenever I'm flooded with compliments on the lines of, 'You speak so well', my heart cuts back to the Colaba apartment...with an empty swing.

A natural-born actor, who has excelled in a wide spectrum of roles—from a ganglord to a maharaja—he has breathed life into strong roles, excelling as Bhiku Mhatre in *Satya*. Known for his serious approach to his craft, his best can be arguably evidenced in *Pinjar, Zubeidaa, Gangs of Wasseypur* and *Shootout at Wadala.*

MANOJ BAJPAYEE

Postcards from Paris

June 1, 1990

Je t'aime.

Yours Sandrine

—

June 10, 1990

Ms Sandrine

Glad to receive postcard from you. Did you mean to send it me? Or was it a mistake? Do you want this card to reach someone else? I am surprised you wrote to my address. My name not there. Just the address. Good to hear from you. Hope you reached safely. How was trip?

Yours Manoj

—

June 19

Darling Manoj

The message is for you *mon cher*. I now offer you its translation. It is simple. But maybe with translation, you understand better. I love you.

Yours Sandrine

—

June 26

Sandrine my dear sweetheart

Really? It is very nice of you. I can't believe. I am happiest man in the world today. I love you too too much. *Je t'aime, je t'aime, je t'aime, je t'aime, je t'aime, je t'aime, je t'aime, je t'aime, je t'aime, je t'aime, je taime. Beaucoup, beaucoup, beaucoup, beaucoup, beaucoup, beaucoup, beaucoup, beaucoup*. This word is difficult to write. I am learning fast your language. It means 'very,' but so many more words *beaucoup* has. I hope you will not mind me calling your goodself sweetheart. You are beautiful, wonderful, lovely, hypnotic, amazing. *Merci merci merci merci. Je t'aime* for all my life, all our lives. Yours mine together. *Beaucoup* kisses.

Manoj

—

July 1

My dearest Manoj

I was very happy *beaucoup* happy receiving your card in which you have returned to me my feelings so beautifully. I am happiest girl in the world today.

My sister gave me the card which she take from the mailbox and it is good she does not read English, but she read French words you wrote. She is my sister Adèle. She is of 12 years. She said something strange. Adèle asked if card was from boyfriend from India. I say control her thoughts. I gave her stamps on the card and she keep silent. She stick stamps in a book and excited to get stamps from India. Stamps of the great Gandhiji. She knows very little things about India, but she knew he was great man who fought for your country's independence with peaceful means.

I do not care if my sister knows about my boyfriend in India, but I be afraid your friends and family not like such things said on a card. Can I call you boyfriend? I like to call you that. You very special. *Beaucoup* special, I laugh here writing this.

I am writing to you inside closed letter today on paper. I have put natural perfume of crushed rose petals on the paper. You smell the roses?

It was superb to be in New Delhi for one month on culture dramatics inter-exchange programme to study drama and acting under Barry John sir. All of us ten students learn lot from M Barry. You are fortunate to be apprentice. We were astonished. He is possessed with knowledge. We were fortunate you there to help us with drama exercises and at improvisation class which were enjoyable. It did not seem like difficult exercise at all. Alain Dupont was jealous of you. He would be little boy when you there. Sulking, I think it is called, not speaking to us after class. Funny Alain. He is handsome no doubt, like Alain Delon, the actor of so many superb films. Therefore, he think all girls like him, no one else is handsome. He is foolish to be silly like this. Nadine, Anna and Beatrice and your Sandrine were all paying much more attention to you. He is getting angry, but he accepted defeat. He can be foolish, but he not bad. He has girlfriend here, they get married next X'mas.

We wish we could have more time in New Delhi. One little month is all time which we were given by programme. I must give you frankness now. I have spent whole two days looking at the French-English dictionary to get spellings and words right to keep in correspondence with you.

If you do not mind, write me a letter next time with paper inside. But please put some beautiful Indian stamps on cover. My sister will like stamps. My English, as I said, is not perfect at all. I hope you do not mind. My Hindi is worse. But I liked that movie name—*Maine Pyar Kiya*. How do you say '*Je t'aime*' in Hindi?

I close with affection. Kisses. I do not know reason, but I am certain we will meet again sooner or later, does not matter. I close also with question: what does love mean to you Manoj? No one can give me answer. Can you?

Sandrine

July 15

Bonjour Sandrine

Sorry I have not written earlier. I also take long time in writing. My English is as bad and good as yours. I come from Bihar. I did not go to English medium school. My English I take time with also with dictionary help. From Hindi to English!

I thought for days about your question and the answer I could write back. What is love? I think every person has own meaning for that. I have not been in love. I respect my parents. They are simple, good people. For them I feel love. I am grateful they have done whatever they could for me. They stay in small village in small house. Sometimes no electricity power.

I went away from home to look for work as actor. It has not been easy. I was rejected from the National School of Drama, very honourable place this. I was lucky Barry sir has given me part-time employment with him. He taught me to lose shyness, change personality, but said I must always remember my past. This past can become my emotional memory.

The first exercise he gave me and which he gave you people also, was to pretend to be a table or chair. You all students from France did that exercise beaucoup well as soon as he told you. To begin with I found it very difficult to become an object while remembering I am human being. With his guidance today I can be any one any thing. A president or an object without life.

Love starts with attraction I think. The minute I saw you, I thought we could be friends, but did not imagined we would be writing like this letters to each other. This is first time I feel that thing called love, but I am afraid also. I am a struggling actor. Dreams only I can have with me. I dream of being on stage, on television, films, wherever I can find chances. I am sure I will be able to do something with my life some day. Presently, I live day to day eating drinking sleeping dreams.

There are so many things to discuss with you. I am flattered you have written me about your true feelings. I have also been honest. From the day you left, you have been with me everywhere I go. Your smile, your talk, walk, your eyes, and your laughter which you never held back. People say I laugh loud all the time. I am like that only. I have found someone who can match my laughter. If I do not make sense, forgive.

The way you laughed when everything was gone wrong at the final dress rehearsal of our play, was not expected. Actors want to be serious all the time without having talent to laugh at mistakes.

People were thinking we would make mess of *Hamlet,* but we put it all together. Did not we? The audience at the Taj Mansingh Hotel was well behaved and silent for once. Otherwise they make lot of noise and are just interested in drinks and food. Public at the plays for Supper Theatre can be very indifferent, totally uninterested. This is one time we captured the audience attention while they were having soup and cutlets! I was feeling so hungry myself. Alain Dupont was not bad as Hamlet, but you were best as Ophelia. That role you were born to play Sandrine.

Waiting for your reply eagerly. Kisses. I feel strange writing about kisses. I have never kissed any girl in my life.

Manoj

—

August 2

Manoj

Just a quick line to say I leaving for Provence for a month. Family takes it vacation there in little house rented for the season. Will write to you from there. Hope you like this postcard—by my favourite artist Renoir. His colours of the French countryside and persons there are so beautiful. You like the card?

Kisses. Do not feel shy Manoj. I will be the first girl you kissing. I do not want to sound like a bad girl, but that is the way I feel really. I promise you kisses.

Sandrine

—

August 10

Renoir postcard was very lovely, *ma chérie*. See I am learning some French. Do not forget me during vacations. I do not want to sound like a bad person also, but I also want to kiss you again and again.

Manoj

—

August 25

Sandrine, no news from you. I hope you are well and keeping in the pink of health. I await your postcard or letter daily, every week. You have become a habit. Good habit, but I beg you to write soon.

Manoj

—

September 10

Sandrine, missing you. You have forgotten me? This postcard you should like. It is a painting by Jamini Roy. You remind me of women in the painting...with deep, black eyes. Kisses.

Manoj

—

September 20

Sandrine, missing you.

Manoj

—

September 30

Are you upset with me or not well? I am worried. Do not forget me.

Kisses from Manoj

—

October 10

Manoj, my dearest dearest ami. I got your wonderful Jamini Roy cards in Provence. They were re-directed to me from Paris. They were delayed. Silly of me. I should given you my vacation home's address.

Please forgive me for my stupidity. I back in Paris now. Our company is middle of planning to stage Hamlet at Opera next month. Our director, Laurent Martin, has given it new meanings by setting it in today's times. I am playing Ophelia all over again. Alain Dupont is Hamlet and is working hard on his performance. He has stopped flirting with the girls. He is funny.

I am enclosing photographs of me in Provence, with my parents and sister Adèle. We had superb time.

Sandrine

—

October 12

I could not believe my ears when you were on telephone last night. I must have dreaming, but it was your voice. Manoj I am truly excited you coming to Paris to see the play performance.

Where you are staying at the pension in Motte-Piquet is not far from my house close to the magnifique Notre Dame. M Barry John is an angel for organisation of your field trip. It is sad you here for five days only, but I show you our wonderful city. You can meet my papa and sister Adèle.

She was collecting your stamps without fail, and says hello to you. I will be at the Charles de Gaulle aeroport to pick you up in my friend's car. I am excited. I will give your first embrace at the *aéroport*...and first kiss at the Notre Dame.

Your Sandrine

—

October 20

Sandrine, this postcard has a view of the Hanging Garden. I have put stamps of Indian flowers on the card for your sister. Say hello back to Adèle for me.

I will be there by Air-India flight on November 10 reaching there at 6.30 a.m. Do not take trouble receiving me at airport. You must be busy with rehearsals. I will find my way to the pension. I carry English-French dictionary guide. With lots of love.

Manoj

—

October 30

I will be at *aéroport* to receive you. No problems. My friend gone to Marseilles. She not available. Alain bring me there in his car. He is also glad to know that you are coming for performance of our play. I have favour to ask. Can you guide him how to throw his voice? He gets very loud at times.

This card of Eiffel Tower was taken from a picture shot by great photographer Marc Riboud. With love... and embrace.

Sandrine

—

November 8

Just five more days I am there with you. Barry sir has lent me his overcoat and gloves to face the winter weather there. See you, darling, at the airport. *Merci beaucoup beaucoup beaucoup beaucoup beaucoup beaucoup beaucoup*. I have written *beaucoup* now seven times. It is a lucky number for me. I saw you first time on April 7 at the airport here. Remember?

Manoj

—

January 10, 1991

Mr Manoj

I am really, truly sorry. You ever forgive me?

Sandrine

—

January 11

Mr Manoj

I pray you to take my phone calls, please. I have to explain.

Sandrine

—

January 14

We can be friends Manoj. I know you it is difficult to understand or forgive me. I ask for once chance to speak.

Sandrine

—

January 15

Please talk with me. Write to me. Please.

—

January 25

Sandrine

I can understand. It is ok. But no point keeping contact. Good luck with your life. *Merci beaucoup* for the time you gave me. Life has to move on.

Manoj

—

February 7

Dearest Manoj

Today is 7th, the number you like. Thank you for your card which proved me that you are going through what I have written to you. You have not torn up my cards. *Merci.*

Manoj, from your point of view, I know I am in wrong. My point of view also shows I am wrong, but I want to say why. Whatever happened—or did not happen—torments me.

This letter—you can smell the crushed rose petals?—will tell you about what I saw our friendship turned out to be. It remained friendship, not love—but we wanted it to be in love. Did we not? Both. I could never give you your first kiss. Not that I did not want to. I felt you did not want me to get close to you. Something hold you back. I did not want to rush you, make the first move as it is said. I kept waiting for your special touch, something little sign to tell me that you wanted to fall in love with me.

At *aéroport,* I see that you were disappointed Alain and our other friends from the inter-exchange programme were there. I could not forbid, helpless to organise any other transport way. I was thinking of taxi, but Beatrice, Nadine, Anna and Alain know you were coming, I could not tell them to keep out. Barry sir wrote to each of all us to look after you.

You went into *pension* at Motte-Piquet smiling, but I know you were not happy. Our promise of first embrace at the *aéroport* could not take place. On behalf of all of us in the repertory I also want to apologise deeply for the manners Alain talked to you during your visit. At the rehearsal at the Opera you advised him, at my request, about his voice pitch. And he insults you. The French seem to think they are champion in everything. He does not realise such generalisations are dangerous. He must not have no business saying, 'You Indian! What you know about acting?' On behalf of all of us, apologies again and forever.

After the play, you and I were not the way we were feeling in our correspondence. We laughed politely, visited the Louvre, Château de Versailles, Montmartre, also the Moulin Rouge since all men like to visit there. For four days, we were together, but as tourist and guide. If you remember, I held your hand at Champs Elysées, put our arms together, but you seemed not comfortable. At the Notre Dame, I wanted to kiss you, but you were aloof and distant. I was sad, 'My dear Manoj is very shy or he is disappointed in me…' Maybe it was wrong to leave it like that. I should have hug you to the heart and kissed you on the street. I wanted to. But I was not sure whether you would like that. My dearest Manoj, I made the first move with '*Je t'aime*' in my first postcard. I wished to do it again, but your coldness prevent me.

Also maybe right or wrong, I imagined Manoj has someone else in life, someone he not told me about. Maybe he is waiting for marriage arranged by family, the way it happens in India. I was not sure. Our kisses remained only on the paper, on postcards and letters.

I am in misery about reaching late at the *aéroport* to see you off back to India. That is where I would have wanted my kisses.

I would have made demand for our love. By the time I reached there, you are gone through immigration clearance gate. I saw you, screamed loud, 'Manoj! Manoj!' but you were upset, did not look back at me. Is it because you did not want to? I am not clear about that.

You leaving without saying 'Goodbye' will trouble me. What did I do wrong, Manoj? If it is because of Alain Dupont that you cut off, that is a pity. Is that the problem Manoj, please let me know.

Till you tell me the reason, I will not rest.

Sandrine

—

March 7

Sandrine

Let us forget problems between us...move on with life. When I met your parents for dinner at your house, they were nice to me. But when you were in the kitchen with your mother and Adèle, your father said casually, 'Sandrine and Alain Dupont have been childhood sweethearts. They are quarreling over small matters, sulk, go out with other people...but this X'mas they get married.'

What more can I say Sandrine? All the best with Alain. He may not be a very good actor, but he will make a very good husband. He adores you from what I make out.

To conclude, may I ask one thing? I wanted to ask this to you in Paris, but didn't. If Alain and you have been childhood sweethearts, why write to me about love? Why did you end up hurting me? Did your father lie to me?

Manoj

—

March 20

Manoj

'Love' is a strange word. Amour est *très étrange,* Manoj. Alain Dupont and I were used to each other, that's all. And no, my father didn't say lie to you. The wedding is for the X'mas week. Before that I imagined to find true love with you. It was not to be. I would have abandoned every thing every one for you.

I feel it is woman's right to make her own mind about who she loves and must wish to marry finally. You did not give me chance to decide. My loss.

I know my father was telling you about Alain. Was that enough reason to discard me? Maybe I expect very much. Maybe it would be different kind of X'mas for me. If you had presented me the first kiss of your life, Manoj, it could have been a *beaucoup, beaucoup, beaucoup, beaucoup, beaucoup, beaucoup, beaucoup different story.*
Au revoir

Sandrine

After a concatenation of feted perfomances in Marathi theatre, he made his mark in cinema with *Ankush, Parinda, Disha, Tiranga, Agni Sakshi* and *Ab Tak Chhapan*. He can be alternately fiery or low-key, virtuous or vicious, and prefers to act in films which test his versatility. Reclusive, he often spends his time in solitude, away from the city, communing with nature in a cut-off coastal township of Maharashtra.

NANA PATEKAR

And father created an actor

A father was stingy with his love for the boy who would be given a second-hand glance, if at all, in the coastal town of Murud. The boy resented the absence of affection. Yet, he was as scared of his father as a traveller is of losing his passport.

Where would the boy go? Why did he have to be in this predicament? Other children weren't. Anger soldered to dread adds up to a strange combination. There's no accurate word to describe this fusion of feelings except to narrate the story of the boy who was denied that love which was surely his birthright.

This story has not been told to date because no one knows or cares about it. Really, why should anyone be interested in a timid rebel? A repressed, restless child? Only the strong and assertive are heroism material, aren't they? Still, your curiosity might be aroused if I make it clear that the story is about a father and a boy whom I knew very closely. The boy, some of you may know. I was that boy.

In Murud, nature's bounty stretched right before my eyes for free, and for that reason, was taken for granted. Murud of the 1950s was not remarkably different than it is today. The Maharasthra coastal town, crowned with the Janjira Fort standing invincibly in the middle of the sea, keeps drawing me back there. Nothing has changed. I'd like to believe neither have I, a boy whose bricks-and-mortar house was sandwiched between an endless quilt of the ocean, a wild forest nurturing thousands of secrets and untold tales of warrior clans, win-or-die battles and impermanent victories. As a child of six or seven, I could see my reflection in the sea, alternately calm and turbulent, mirroring my moods. At a touch away, the forests were sanctuaries for animals, snakes and birds, great and small, friendly and dangerous.

Dangerous, but not as forbidding as Gajanand Laxman Patekar, a small-framed man elated by the nation's freedom from the British Raj. A vegetarian, teetotaller, non-smoker, he would recoil at the scent of cakes because eggs are included in their ingredients. In height, he resembled a sapling which had stopped growing—only 5' 3". At home, he wore a starched white shirt over a *dhoti*. When he left for work, he wore a Gandhi *topi* over a head full of curly hair, just like his son's. A dark cotton waistcoat completed the patriarch's uniform. Throughout the week, he would be in Bombay where he owned a printing factory, besides trucks, and two cars—an Ambassador and a Fiat. Over weekends, he would return to the Murud house, emerging from the forest pathways to spend the evenings with his wife and children on their home's verandah.

More accurately, I should say to spend time with my mother and my youngest brother, Dilip, whom he adored, demonstrating that with hugs, kisses and conversations in sing-song gibberish. My mother, Anasuya, doted on Dilip too, tossing me a benign sentence occasionally, 'Nana, come have your dinner or it'll get cold.' That wasn't sufficient; they weren't doing me a favour by giving me food to eat and a paper-thin mattress to sleep on. That's the least they could do. In fact, I wasn't sure whether my parents loved me at all. Another brother had been handed over to one of my uncles who had no children, a tradition which was quite common then. I'm surprised I wasn't parcelled off to the uncle. Perhaps the uncle had refused to accept me. I'm not sure. Neither do I want to be.

The youngest child was treasured: Dilip was beautiful, fair-skinned, well-behaved, angelic. I was the complete opposite, possessing none of those qualities. For tiny errors and, at times, no errors, I would be slapped hard across the face, and told to behave or else I would be tossed into the sea. For a child, that can conjure up terrifying visuals.

The reasons for Gajanand Laxman Patekar's prejudice left me as angry as the monsoon rains lashing our Murud home. I believed thunder and lightning were a sign from God for my parents: 'Don't be like that with your boy. Mend your ways. Or I'll blow your house away with the next storm. Don't tempt me.' God kept threatening my father and I felt chuffed that at least God was on my side even if he wasn't putting his threats into practice. I wasn't overreacting; I wasn't paranoid.

Dilip was the *gora* one, I the *kala* one. More than the complexion issue, Dilip would never use any other word, but,

'Yes.' I wouldn't use any other word, but 'No.' I would be given Dilip's leftovers; he got the first serving at meals. New cricket bats would be bought from the Mumbai markets for him. I simmered like dying embers, with envy. I must have developed an inferiority complex because of step-parental treatment, but I didn't indulge in self-pity. I wouldn't cry. That's me right till today—I have been self-trained in storing my tears within.

'I hope he doesn't beat me up,' I would seethe, 'because I'll beat him back.' To avoid violent conflicts, I would hide behind a door as soon as I saw my father enter the house on Saturday afternoons. His patented words would echo in my ears, '*Kya re, kya tu*...what are you doing? You good-for-nothing fellow.' That stung. Even if Dilip was gaping at a wall, he would be mollycoddled, 'Good boy, good boy. I know you will do me proud.'

'No, Dilip will not,' spitefully, I would tell the ocean. 'I will show that man. He will have to eat his words; he will apologise to me some day. Before he can provoke me...that I am worthless, I'll show him that I'm the best son anyone could give birth to. And then let's see. If he admits that he has been wrong, I won't accept his apologies. I will ignore him the way he's ignoring me, a little boy who's so desperate to be his son.'

I must have been eight or nine years old in the fifth or sixth standard of a Marathi-medium school when it staged its annual play. It was on the life of Valmiki, the highway thief who atoned for his sins by writing the great epic, Ramayana. My father returned to Murud to see me in the play and that too, on a weekday. Odd. He had never cared even if I was in bed raging with 102° temperature. At the end of the show, I was shocked. He had tears in his eyes. For the first time, I felt the warmth of his embrace. He was over the moon. His son had redeemed himself; he had acted on stage. So what if it was only in the role of one of Valmiki's henchmen?

It was a denied sensation. I felt like Gajanand Laxman Patekar's son. He had, believe it or don't, accepted me in public...as if in a day I had become the town's Natya Samrat. My school friends and teachers were witnesses to his generosity; now he could never deny me the love of a father. I would not have to hide behind doors anymore. To retain his affection, I would have to act on stage, whenever and wherever I could. From that moment, I could not stop acting. I was part of the world he admired—theatre. He was an enthusiast of the performing arts, a regular at *tamashas*, *nautankis* and classical musical recitals. *Tamasha* producers and the artistes called him Dada. He regarded theatre and music as an exalted realm for the divinely talented. The way to his heart, I understood, was to act for the rest of my life.

I had become as adorable as Dilip, who didn't mind sharing our parents' love from that day onwards. Sibling rivalry, or whatever it is termed, had tormented me till that annual play in school. Dilip was too good to be true, chirruping like a sparrow, when we returned home that day, triumphant. Valmiki's henchman had brought honour to the family.

A generalisation goes that parents realise their frustrated dreams through their children. That's sham psychology. My father did not harbour any repressed desires. He relished the performing arts; he didn't want to be one of their participants. He could appreciate a classical vocal recital without secretly wishing that he could be the artiste. He saw himself as the creator of an artiste. In the event, I had to act whenever and wherever I could to sustain my father's appreciation.

Murud was a dream-run till my father was cheated by his business partners. Instances of trustworthy friends securing signatures on documents were commonplace in the 1950s. My father was aware of this, but in a weak moment, signed his business away to his partners whom he thought he could trust with his life. Such cheats receive their comeuppance eventually: the partners didn't survive in the trade beyond a couple of years. They died. Betrayal wreaks its own vengeance.

Still, Ganjanand Laxman Patkar was shattered beyond recovery, retreating into a shell, like a tortoise. From the serenity of Murud, we moved to the pandemonium of Bombay. A small-town boy is expected to be awestruck by a big city. I did not have the luxury to indulge in awe: I had to work and I did, feeling even superior and high and mighty compared to the kids I saw going to school in cars and buses. I stuck film posters on the city's walls from afternoon to 1 at night, walking a stretch of 16 kilometres every day. From the factories at Chunabhatti to housing colonies in the folds of Opera House and the shopping centres of Colaba, I would stick posters on the walls on my beat, posters that were rough, duplicated and triplicated versions of the originals for *Tiger Don, From Cairo with Love, That Man in Istanbul,*

Tiger Prepares Dynamite. Perhaps unknowingly, I wanted to become one of those gun-wielding heroes with a voluptuous woman by my side. Poster-pasting earned me a meal and ₹40 a week, which wasn't bad back then; it was sufficient for a family's rations.

Dilip worked at an office in Opera House. The brothers had become the bread-earners. My mother's family had quite a few relatives in the underworld, but she had broken all ties with them. If I picked up a quarrel with anyone—and my temper was always straining at the leash—she would warn me, 'Do you want to become like one of your useless uncles and those cousins?'

Meanwhile, my father continued to brood. I heard him say, 'I gave so much to others, but I haven't been able to give anything to our children. I was unfair…' He would offer us superfluous advice, 'Sons, never borrow or lend any money. If you do borrow money, give back ₹20 for ₹10.' No one lends money without a usurious rate of interest. Who was to tell him? For him, I acted with troupes, fired by their passion for pure theatre. My parents also hoped that I would, by some miracle, complete college studies. For me that meant the JJ School of Arts. I graduated in commercial art and found employment with an ad agency. Simultaneously, I acted in progressive Marathi plays like *Mahasagar, Pahije Jatiche* and *Hamidabaichi Kothi*.

After a show of Vijaya Mehta's *Hamidabaichi Kothi*, my father came backstage. Before he could spot me among the crowd in the green room, Vijaya*bai* asked him who he was and he said he wanted to see his son Nana. To that Vijaya*bai* said instinctively, 'But he's my son...not yours.' My father would quote that often; he thrilled that his son had an extended family in theatre.

By now I was earning ₹250 a show, the highest sum paid to a theatre actor then. The family did not have to worry about its rations any longer. I did not have to worry about losing my father's love...ever. He passed away before I achieved recognition as a film actor. He saw my film *Gaman*, but couldn't quite understand what it was all about. He liked stories which were told simply, with an emotional underlining just like his own personality.

He was a man whose love became even more intense, when he was anxious about his son. I must have been twelve or thirteen when a cyst developed on my hand. Dr Irani of 14th Lane, Khetwadi, diagnosed it as cancerous. While walking to Grant Road railway station to catch a train for Matunga, my father stopped at the fruit market and bought two apples. In the train, he gave me one of the apples and said, 'You must eat well. Also promise me—don't think about what the doctor said. He's a fool. He's growing old, talking of cancer and stuff. One more promise...don't tell your mother what that silly doctor said. She'll worry.'

I ate the apple. He wiped my mouth with the back of his palm and smiled the warmest smile I had ever received from him in my life.

Around 1979, my father was admitted to KEM Hospital because of a heart ailment. Those who are gentle and caring have to deal with their hearts, I suppose. I was away shooting in the interiors of Maharashtra for the Marathi film *Nagin*. A trunk call informed the unit that Nana's father is no more. They didn't tell me that. To keep me under control, they asked me to leave for Mumbai right away. It was only on reaching home that I saw the emptiness. He had left.

Today I am sixty-one years old, but regard myself as the child whose father made him experience extremes—from indifference to limitless love. These qualities can become lethal weapons for an actor if he's sufficiently skilled to diagnose the reasons. There's no point in denying either of these extremes. Those who believe that they are self-made are lousy actors. Those who accept that they apply what they have experienced in their private lives before the public are honest. I do not grade myself as a lousy or an honest actor. That would be so easy; only insecure actors do that. But I do remind myself, if my father had not applauded me—his two small hands put together—I would have still been sticking posters on the city's walls.

Two or three years ago, when my mother turned ninety-four, I had a portrait painted of my father. I held it close to her eyes and she looked at it curiously. Then she folded her five fingers into a kiss, touched the portrait and then my face. 'Isn't that you Nana? You're looking good,' she said.

I didn't contradict her. Because Gajanand Laxman Patekar and I are inseparable. I act only for his applause.

Trained at New Delhi's hallowed National School of Drama, he began with small but significant parts in films spawned by the gutsy parallel cinema of the 1970s. With *Ardh Satya, Aakrosh, Jaane Bhi Do Yaaro* and *Aarohan,* he was acknowledged as one of the finest Indian actors, endowed with a deep, expressive voice. He has been seen in top-notch international productions, over the years, under the helmsmanship of such directors as Mike Nichols and Roland Joffe. A character actor, today he enhances the value of film projects ranging from the typically Bollywood to the defiantly unconventional.

OM PURI

The kindness of strangers

Stories can be our most priceless possession. We usually remember the most painful ones, or the most pleasurable. The past defines our present. There are many stories to tell, so many that they leap to my mind suddenly, just as I thought they were long forgotten, dead and buried.

To organise the stories and narrate them coherently, separately or all together in a book as a novel, is a writer's skill and talent. Even if one were to fictionalise the stories—add fantasy, subtract reality—they are a reflection of one's personality. Those who erase the past are fortunate, they do not carry the burden. At the same time, they lose an important part of themselves by going into denial mode.

For this story, I chose a mosaic of characters, absolute or virtual strangers, who had nothing to gain from me. There was only give, but little or no take. When I look back at my story, it is that of an actor who, like so many others, struggled hard during his initial years and ultimately found his calling, not because of that thing called destiny, but because of the kindness of strangers.

We either romanticise our childhood and youth, or look back with disaffection about the conditions we were born into. While telling this story, I can be dispassionate, what is called 'objective', albeit to a degree.

My parents, TC Puri and Tara Devi, were opposites. He, a ticket collector with the railways, was given to mood swings. She was a kind-hearted soul, religious and practical. We would move homes frequently because my father would be transferred to different places. In fact, he had this talent for getting into trouble. An angry man in his youth, he was suspended for six months following the theft of cement gunny bags from a railway storeroom.

To start with, he could not afford to educate me. As a six-year-old, I washed glasses and plates at a tea shop in Bhatinda. Then I got myself a promotion—washing utensils at a *dhaba*. After that, I was sent to stay with my maternal uncle in Sanaur, Patiala, where I was actually enrolled in a school.

There would be tension at my uncle's house. My father did not get along with him, coaxing my mother to insist on a share of the property from her side of the family. By the time I was in the ninth standard, I was paying for my own fees by giving tuitions; I guess I was brighter than most at studies. And by the time I was in the first year of college, my mother passed away after lying in a coma for twenty days. She gave up on life, just like that.

I aspired to act in theatre, study at the National School of Drama in New Delhi. But where and how would I live and subsist in the Capital city?

One day, on an impulse, I walked into Punjab House, which is directly in front of Mandi House, a walk away from the NSD. Perhaps I could rustle up some money for paying-guest accommodation. The clerk at the reception counter said, 'Sorry, not possible at all.' Then just as I was about to make my exit, he asked, raising his voice, 'What do you do, young man?'

'I'm a student. Can I just stay here for fifteen to twenty days till I find a room somewhere?'

'Okay,' he said. 'There's a storeroom besides the kitchen. Will that be okay with you?'

'Absolutely.'

Sudeep Chakravarty became a lifelong friend. He was interested in theatre, he would talk non-stop about plays and acting for the years I ended up staying in the storeroom. Today, he has retired from his clerical job and runs a theatre group in Lucknow. Sudeep directs plays. Our conversations were all the rent I paid him.

Strangers, all without exception, we are brought up to believe, are to be distrusted, but in this case, it was sheer instinct which forged a friendship that changed the course of both our lives.

At the NSD, Naseeruddin Shah suggested that I follow up the study in drama, by joining him at the Film and Television Institute of India, Pune. How? Neelam Mansingh of Delhi, who was at the forefront of the theatre movement, introduced me to an industrialist at a party. She had spoken to him about subsidising me at the Film Institute. He agreed to help me with a monthly stipend of ₹300, a princely sum those days, but just about enough to pay the academic fees. The industrialist ended our conversation with a *non sequitur* that evening.

'Do you smoke?'

'Yes,' I replied uncertainly. And he immediately handed over a packet of State Express 555 cigarettes.

I suppose he was making me feel posh. Cigarettes accepted, as long as the stipend saw me though the Film Institute studies. Once at Pune, the hostel provided the roof. As for meals, I hit a blank till the manager of the mess, Chitale sir, played Good Samaritan.

'At the mess, we serve a hundred students. We can afford to feed the hundred-and-first free,' Chitale said, without a hint at charity, but apologised, 'Don't worry about your lunch and dinner. They're on the house. Breakfast, you have to organise for yourself.'

Tea and bread were affordable, and other students would help out too. All was well till the industrialist's money stopped. I was informed that no more aid would come, and to interpret that anyway I wanted to. Deadlock. Now what? My debts piled up at the institute's office. As it happened, I seemed to impress the faculty and the institute's chief at that time, NVK Murthy. The accounts department's peon would remind me of the money I owed, gently not belligerently. By the time I graduated and was about to leave the campus, Murthy waived off the debts, probably paying the amount himself without letting me know about it.

I wasn't bitter about the sudden closure of the stipend from the industrialist. It gave me a kickstart. Add to that Naseer's persuasion, it was like being thrown into the deep end of film acting. I learnt to swim and survive. The tide remained choppy.

I set out in the quest of film roles, I travelled to Mumbai, aware that finding a room there was as impossible as finding God. I was an unwanted guest at several homes, for a day, sometimes day and night, till there was no alternative but to seek shelter at the Ganga Vihar apartment of Rani Burra, also from the Film Institute. Rani was a helpful sort, but how many could she fit into the rooms blessed with a sea-facing view of Marine Drive. Girish Karnad, BV Karanth and Kulbhushan Kharbanda were already there. In her typical drawl, Rani said, 'Okaaaay, let's see what can be done. You can be here for a few days maybe.' The few days turned out to be one-and-a-half long years. If I couldn't pay the token rent she charged, she never brought it up.

I am not particularly gregarious. Perhaps I received kindness for being unpretentious. They didn't need any confirmation that I was an actor who did not fit into the conventional mould of Hindi cinema, but things were changing. A new kind of cinema was being made, which defied the song-and-dance formula. Naseer and I happened to look for opportunities to act at the right place and at the right time. It was as if things were happening naturally, in keeping with the shifts of style and content in cinema the world over.

Roles, small or big, came to me, and I grabbed them with both hands. Life was looking up. *Ardh Satya,* in which Govind Nihalani had assigned me the lead role, turned out to be a success. And that's when my father gave me a resounding slap across the face, for the second time in my life.

The first time I can understand. I had sided with my mother when he was arguing with her. He was in such a temper that he kicked the *angeethi* on which she was cooking *daal*. And then he slapped me so hard that I went flying. His hands are as huge and powerful as Dharmendra's in the movies.

I never forgot that slap. Never. But the second slap was unexpected. I had returned home in the evening to my flat in Andheri where he was staying with me, and he was in a rage all over again. Some neighbours had been talking to him, poisoning his ears that although *Ardh Satya* was a hit and was, in fact, quite like *Zanjeer*, it had not made me a superstar overnight. Amitabh Bachchan, after *Zanjeer*, was a superstar. 'But look at your son,' they had badgered. 'Does he get the same kind of money?'

His son, TC Puri felt, wasn't doing right, he was content with peanuts. He took one long look at me when I entered the house, and gave me one tight slap right across the face. I went flying. It didn't stop there, he caught hold of my collar and almost throttled me. I left home.

For three days I didn't dare to return. Where could I go? To whoever could give me shelter, and that turned out to be a friend's house close by in a Lokhandwala colony. I wasn't asked why I had left home. I was given the courtesy to be with myself and my thoughts. I came to the conclusion that this is the way it is, accept it. My father has a certain attitude towards life, and I have mine.

Such little stories live within me. With time, the pain has distilled into pleasure. Life can be beautiful once you've accepted the fact that this is the way it is.

At home, most of all, in roles which have a credible, contemporary edge, he was described by *Time* magazine as 'the superstar of Indian arthouse cinema.' From *Thakshak, English, August, Bombay Boyzz, Mr and Mrs Iyer* to the phantasmagorically mounted *Vishwaroopam,* he's an actor who craves creative derring-do. A social activist, a sportsperson, a voracious reader and quite the protean Mumbaikar, he went behind the camera to direct the tremendously undervalued *Everybody Says I'm Fine.*

RAHUL BOSE

Rugby paradiso

I should have quit. As the opposition flanker's fist hit my nose and blood spurted out in neat arcs, I should have quit playing rugby. I should have realised rugby and an acting career as a leading man do not go together. I should have walked away. It didn't pay, no one watched it, and India wasn't even recognised as an official rugby-playing nation. Instead, I got the nose reset by Dr Narendra Pandya, a man whom I was destined to meet many times in my life thereafter, but didn't know that yet, and presented myself in front of Dev Benegal, the director of *English, August*.

It was Dev's debut feature as a director, and after many months of searching for the actor who'd play the protagonist, Agastya Sen, he'd selected me. The audition process had been pretty interesting. The first time he'd put me on camera, I had to lie down (on a bean bag), mumble a few lines and simulate masturbation. Evidently I did that pretty well (I had practised hard for it), well enough to make it to the next round. That had consisted of mumbling very many lines (Agastya only mumbled, he was cool) with the entire cast straining to hear what the hell I'd said. Finally, in the last round I had to have sex with Dev. Which would have definitely taken less time than the actual session of acting, and the improvising which we ended up doing. So there I was, six months later, a week away from acting in my first feature, with two black eyes and a swollen nose in plaster. I stood guiltily in front of Dev. At first he didn't recognise me. When he did, he tried hard to control himself.

'What happened?' His voice was starched and tight.

'Well...,' I tried to think of something plausible and non-rugby.

'Rugby, right?'

I stared at his shadow. It had torn itself away from his body and was advancing towards me.

'Yup, rugby. I broke my nose,' I mumbled nasally.

The shadow threw itself and began to punch me.

'Ah. And how long will it take to heal?'

'Six weeks. For all the scarring to go.'

Bludgeoning me to the ground, Shadow took out a thin wire from its pocket and proceeded to strangulate me.

'But filming's a week away.'

'I know, Dev. Sorry.'

Jumping all over my unconscious body, Shadow ran to the kitchen to get a chopper.

I screamed, 'I'm sorry! I'll give up the game! I mean it!'

I didn't. Nor did Dev. Shoot the next week, that is. He waited and made *English, August* with me. While this is a story of the eternal conflict between my film and my rugby career, I'm not making a case for martyrdom here. No one forced me to do both; I chose to, year after year. I forget the number of times my father and sister sat me down, pleading into my newly bandaged face, 'Rahul, learn from this injury.' There is a very good reason why the number of actors who are international rugby players, totals…one. I would nod and swear today's game was the last one of my life. I might even have stopped after arthroscopies on both my knees before I was two left me wondering whether the sport was worth so much pain and frustration. That's when, in '98, three years after the successful release of *English, August*, India was officially recognised as a rugby-playing nation by the International Rugby Board. I now had a very good chance of playing for the country. Playing for India! Wearing the India blazer with the Ashok Chakra emblazoned on it. Playing in different countries with the tricolour aloft and the National Anthem surging through the stadium. Playing at home, at the Bombay Gymkhana, my home ground, with thousands of spectators screaming, egging us on. There was no way I wasn't going to try. I plunged in.

Looking back, things moved so fast, they're almost a blur. One day we were boys playing hard, but nowhere near professional, at the Bombay Gymkhana grounds, and the next, the entire scenario had changed. The Board had allocated funds for the national team, appointed a national coach, and organised national training camps. The latest equipment, training methods and countrywide selection meant this was serious stuff. And then, before I knew it, it was October 14, 1998. India was playing its first official rugby international against Singapore at the National Stadium. I had made it to the Indian team.

It was a warm evening in Singapore. The stadium was pretty full, crowds having come in to cheer the home team. We stood in the starting line-up, stamping our feet, clapping our hands, twitching with the tension of our first international game. And then it happened. The moment that has since become the favourite memory of my eleven-year-long international career. The National Anthem started. We stared up at the Indian flag and I remember thinking—not more than a handful of Indians know the sport, leave alone that India has a national team. And yet here we are, here I am, the India crest on my jersey, playing for a country that has made me everything I am, a country whose soil is a thing of magic, it's heat inside my soul. So whether the rest of India knew whether if we were playing or not, I would play with everything I have. I would, as our coach used to exhort us, 'leave my body on the field.' Almost predictably, we lost and badly at that. But we were on our way. At 98th in the world, we were on the world rugby map. Soon the intensity ramped up exponentially. The next year's international calendar of fixtures looked really exciting, but how was I to juggle films with my fledgeling career as an international sportsperson?

It was 1999, absolutely the wrong time to give my film career a break. Wisely, I didn't. That year was the first of many during which I juggled my two lives. Two crack offers had come my way and I was damned if I was going to turn them down. Govind Nihalani had signed me on to play the psychotic Sunny in *Thakshak,* and Dev had offered me the lead in *Split Wide Open*. I lied to both about 'family issues' and 'court cases', which had to be sorted out at coincidentally the same time India was playing rugby tournaments, and swung schedules that fitted. It was a fantastic twelve months. I did *Thakshak,* my first film in Hindi, sweating over pages of dialogue Mr Nihalani insisted I perfect. But it was worth it. Playing a manic, complex, self-obsessed sociopath, Sunny, it's a bit worrying how fondly I think of him fifteen years later, because God, he was pure evil. I shot AK Hangal and Amrish Puri (may their souls rest in peace) in cold blood in the film. Brilliant! I threw my sweet friend, Atul Kumar, off a tenth floor balcony in the pre-climax scene. What fun! I even got to kiss the hapless Nethra Raghuraman full on the lips, in my second screen kiss. The first had been a month before with the impossibly beautiful Laila Rouass in *Split Wide Open*. Anyone who kisses Laila Rouass would never forget the moment, but I remember the scene particularly vividly, not for the kiss, but what preceded it. It's the part where rich NRI, Laila, who is illicitly attracted to slum boy, KP, goes to check out the slum where he stays. It turns out that KP shares a room with another in a boat which is being repaired. Once there, she seduces him, slowly stripping down to her underwear. Maddened with lust, KP violently kisses her and they both rip off his clothes till he is naked. She then walks around him appraising his equipment. Finally she says, 'Not bad,' and the scene cuts away while they presumably have steamy sex inside the boat. Not the easiest scene to shoot. If being butt-naked in front of a stranger is unthinkable, imagine stripping down in front of a film crew. That was the first time I used a crotch pad. A triangle of cloth, it sticks on to the stomach and thighs with tape. So if, as it was in this case, the camera is behind you, it gives the impression you are totally naked, letting me preserve some secrets from Laila. But that wasn't the fun part. The fun part was the first kiss. Laila and I discussed how, for it to work, it had to be animalistic, hungry, almost feral. Cameras rolled, Dev called for action, Laila started saying her lines, I grabbed her and yanked her on to me. Our mouths slammed, our teeth clashed and we began to eat each other alive. Dev called, 'Cut' and from his upbeat tone I knew the kiss had worked. What I didn't know was the clash of teeth had chipped one of Laila's. She showed me the broken piece, stared at me for long while I shifted about uneasily (totally naked, remember), suddenly aware how vulnerable I was, and then said, 'I hope, for your sake, there isn't a second take.' There wasn't.

But there certainly was a second season of international rugby for me. By now the Indian Army was on board and the Indian Rugby Football Union began teaching the forces the sport. The national coach, Willy Hetaraka, a New Zealander of Maori descent, was sent to the Army regimental centre in Ahmednagar to teach the *jawans*. 'I was getting ready to conduct my first session with the army lads,' he would recount to me years later, 'when a few of them came to me and said something was wrong with all the rugby balls I had brought. They had pumped and pumped air into them for all they were worth, but the balls had remained oval in shape. "What to do Willy sir?" they asked despondently. There wasn't one round ball in the kit. Should they get a football from their stores? You had to be there to see the disbelief in their eyes when I explained rugby was played with an oval ball.' The Army boys learned hard and learned fast. By 2003, a few of them had made the Indian team. And what an Indian team that was. It took the cliché, 'glorious diversities make up this wonderful country' and magnified it till it hit you square in the eyeballs. We had two farmers from Haryana, a truck driver from Chennai, an NRI *sardar* from Birmingham, a student from Manipur, Army *jawans* from Punjab and Rajasthan, Maharashtrian policemen from the Greater Mumbai Police, and six of us posh, South Bombay schools-educated boys with public school accents. Add to that, Francis, a snow-white English boy who, under the Union rules, was eligible to play for India because his grandfather had been born here. Training was conducted in six languages. It would start with Willy's Kiwi-accented English, transform into Indian-accented English for the boys from the south and northeast, then get translated into Hindi, which would then be broken down into Haryanvi, Marathi and Punjabi.

Like American football, rugby has set plays, calls and manoeuvres. Willy would watch with bemusement as his complex codes would be morphed into a rough, pidgin language to make it comprehensible to the entire team. So a lineout throw-in code '41789alpha4362metrobombay', would be translated into Hindi as, 'Parminder *ke liye, phir* Maruti' ('ball to Parminder, then we drive/push as a pack'). Why sweat the small stuff, we figured; none in the opposition knew Hindi. It was this team that began to tour the Asia-Pacific region for zonal tournaments. Our opening foreign tour of the season was the first time many of our boys had passports. The first time they were staying in a five-star hotel. The first time they were eating food that was not Indian. The first time they had ever seen...toilet paper. So it was one morning during the team's blackboard session, that we were looking for some pen and paper to draw out a few moves when one of the Haryanvi farmers brought out a wad of toilet paper and offered it to us. When we explained what he had given us, his face cleared. 'Ah,' he said. That's what it was there for. He had wondered why there were no *lota*s and taps next to the WC. How then had he cleaned himself, we asked him. He hadn't, he replied happily. He had just pulled up his shorts and come for the meeting. It was our fastest blackboard session with everyone out of the door in seconds. Only later did he tell us he was joking. He had asked his roommate who had told him what the paper was meant for. Even so, he said, it left him feeling dirty so he showered after, just to be on the safe side.

Meanwhile, I don't know if it was the euphoria of playing for India that was rubbing off on to my film career or just one of those fortunate phases, but I had signed *Mr and Mrs Iyer*, *Jhankaar Beats* and *Chameli*. For the role of Rishi, the drummer in the band vying to become Jhankaar Beats champions, the producers found a young man staying in a priory in Prarthna Samaj, who owned a drum set and had offered to teach me. Every day he would quietly go mad as I drummed all rhythm out of his head. Finally I mastered the boom-boom bam! boom-boom bam! of 'We will, we will rock you...' *Jhankaar* was liberating. It was my first broad comedy and working with the irrepressibly eccentric Sujoy Ghosh was infuriating and joyous in equal measure. Infuriating because he had an idea a minute and didn't see why they couldn't all be a part of the movie, and joyous because he remains one of the funniest, well-meaning people I know with no trace of ego. It was a massive relief that Sujoy knew and loved rugby. Having grown up in England, he had played the sport and understood my passion for it. This was the first director I didn't have to lie to about my unavailability on some dates because they clashed with a game. This was the first director who would quietly let me off early from filming so I could make it for a match.

Which brings me to the flip side of things. How did my teammates react to my film career? What did they make of me signing autographs for reasons which had nothing to do with rugby? The answer lies in two parts. The first time I raced to a game straight from a shoot, as usual the atmosphere was tense, quiet. Boys were getting massaged on the therapist's table, some were being strapped by the physio, others were rubbing Ben-Gay over sore muscles. Two of our biggest lads were getting their necks stretched out by the assistant physio, a few of our quickest were applying Vaseline to their boots (so that mud would not stick to them), while our flankers quietly boiled their new mouth guards. In the midst of all this, I began to take my make-up off with cleanser, gently sloughing my face in upward strokes and using wet wipes with care and precision. As I began to work with an ear-bud tipped with a dot of cleansing milk to take out the eye pencil colour around my eyes, I became aware of being stared at. I looked around. The room was absolutely still. Everyone was looking at me trying to figure out what I was up to. Finally the captain walked up to me, gazed into my face smeared with eye colour and said, 'I don't know what the fuck you're doing, but if you don't get kitted out in the next five minutes, you're off the team.' From then on the team became pretty blasé about it. It was, 'Bose is doing his gay thing.' (Yup, rugby boys aren't very up on gender politics).

The second half of the answer's a little more complex. Fact: I was a good rugby player, but not a great one. I had fitness, mental strength, a rugby brain and the right technique, but I wasn't a genius. I was not a star on the Indian team and I had to fight hard to make the squad. I was accorded ordinary treatment during training, strategy sessions and matches. I ate with the team, rode the team bus and did team duty like everyone else. It was the time in-between that things would suddenly change. After a match in a national tournament where I had performed well, but not spectacularly, I would walk off the field in relative anonymity, but just as I'd cross over from the playing area to the grounds outside, the requests for autographs, photographs and 'Can you please speak to my sister on the phone? She is a big fan,' would start. My own teammates, who would never think of asking me for a photograph on account of my rugby skills, would blush and ask me to pose with them. Aggressive Haryanvi farmer, surly Tamilian truck driver, they were all the same, grinning madly into the camera, arms around me. Then the jokes would start. How I acted to fake an injury, how I refused to tackle someone because my precious face would be injured, etc., etc.

And so eleven years flew by in this delicate dance between playing the world's most violent outdoor sport and working in a profession in which looks are everything. In between, I'd stopped to have 180 pieces of stone embedded in the corneas of my eyes swabbed off by a shaken ophthalmic surgeon, who told me I was two millimetres away from partial blindness. I had my eyebrow microsutured with nine internal and eleven external stitches by the redoubtable Dr Pandya. My nose was reset for the third time with the warning that if it happened again 'no doctor will be able to do anything'. Eleven years of playing with boys who were young enough to be my children (When I told a nineteen-year-old India debutant I was forty, he almost collapsed. His mother was forty-one). Eleven years of learning calm under pressure from rugby and applying it to directing *Everybody Says I'm Fine!*, of learning patience and not losing concentration during filming and applying it to a tense final that went into sudden death. Eleven years of slowly ascending the world rankings till we reached 83rd when I retired.

My last international was against Pakistan in Bangkok. I had the honour of leading the previous night's training session. A lot of jokes about, 'At last the old man is getting the message' flew around the ground. The next day we won 92-0. That night was epic. Many beers, many cheers, many tears. The next morning, I flew back to Mumbai and on to Sunderbans to shoot what would turn out to be my most satisfying role to date in *The Japanese Wife*. I reached the hotel, gave Aparna Sen a hug and the first thing she said was, 'At last you're done with that dreadful game.' If only it were that simple. Rugby is a drug.

No matter how many times you break your nose, no matter how many times you holler with pain, no matter how many times you sit at home with frozen gel packs on your face, you know you will return to take your place under a hot, summer sky, arms around the shoulders of a teammate, the smell of Ben-Gay and the sound of claps rippling around you. To glory in a joy so elemental, but known to so few. The joy of running with a ball in your hand and beating destiny.

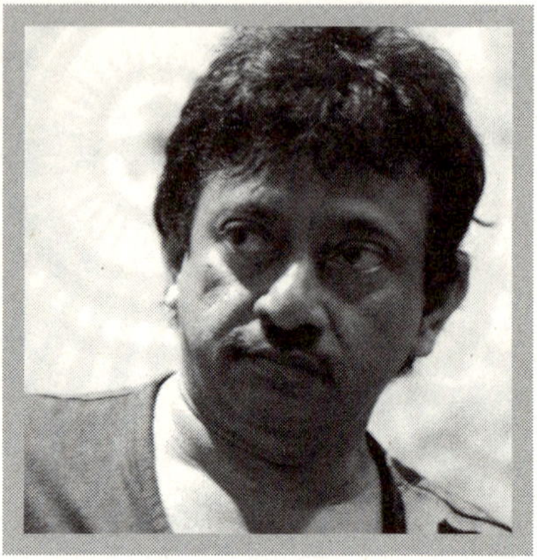

A man of surprises, the Hyderabad-domiciled director and producer shifted to Mumbai, but belted out unconventional films in Hindi as well as Telugu. He is immune to tags like 'rogue thinker' and 'maverick', bestowed upon for his immense oeuvre, the highpoints including *Shiva, Rangeela,* the trend-setting *Satya* followed up by *Bhoot, Company, Sarkar* and *Rakta Charitra*. He is bemused about *Ram Gopal Varma ki Aag*—a remake of *Sholay*—which was loathed by the mandarins as well as the masses. Nothing can furrow the brows of this brand name, as long as he can continue making cinema on his own terms.

RAM GOPAL VARMA

The boy who didn't laugh or cry

This story is about a little boy trying to open the wooden gate of his house in Hyderabad, and not being able to. This was in the middle class Punjagutta Colony where he lived most of his life. Now he owns an apartment in Srinagar Colony, but can never forget that wooden gate which wouldn't open.

His family hailed from a Kshatriya lineage, not that it made much difference to him. His maternal grandmother was a scholarly Ram *bhakt*. He remembers little else about the virtues of his grandparents.

His father, Krishnan Raju Penumatsa, was a sound engineer at Sarathy and then at Annapurna Studio. The best quality about the father was that he would let his three children do anything they wanted to. The boy, having difficulty with the wooden gate, looked up to his father although they didn't interact much. Neither expressed the need for a cuddle or a warm embrace. Truth be told, the father—a typically humble man who would travel to the studio on an old Vespa scooter—did not exercise sufficient, if any, control over his two sons and a daughter, which was thought to be very wrong then, especially in the case of the eldest son. Now everyone agrees that he was so right to give the boy the freedom to shape his own life. The father was sixty-five when he passed away. He didn't drink much, but he was a heavy smoker, into three packets a day.

The boy, it could be said, had a very normal childhood. The problem was that he was a very abnormal child. More playful than could be tolerated, he would derive some strange pleasure from not doing his school homework. His mother would beat him up a lot with *chappals* when she couldn't find a leather belt. The boy was either a bad child or she was a bad mother! Seriously, he gave her grief by insisting on doing his own thing. At St Mary's School and then at New Science College, he was a backbencher, lost in his own world. He was not interested in studies; text books would bore the pants off him. Naturally, he would flunk twice over at the tenth standard exams, and had to repeat his Intermediate exams as well as BE civil engineering exams.

Incidentally, playfulness for him meant playing hide and seek, at times with his own imagination. He did not mind being alone; he would hide behind a tree and whoop with joy on finding himself. He would also retreat into a kingdom of comics: Casper the Friendly Ghost, Wendy the Witch, Little Lotta, Lulu, Tarzan and Phantom. He couldn't relate to Superman, Batman or Spiderman. He still can't. The invulnerable and the unbelievable don't interest him.

At high school, he tried to get into the cricket team because that's what all the kids were supposed to do. He must have been fourteen or fifteen when a cricket ball hit his knee. He was hurt, upset...why should a game inflict pain? That's why he hates cricket, doesn't know the difference between one-day and Test matches.

His mother gave up on him; his father was a shadow, working crazy hours at the studio. The schoolboy started hanging out with street gangs. He would get into turf wars, like dogs do when they see another group of dogs encroaching on their space. Street wars would break out, but he was smart enough to remain at the back of the fights involving fists and hockey sticks. And of course, if he saw his gang was getting thrashed, he would make a run for it. Chicken-hearted? Sure.

The concept of a regimented education baffled him. Why should he understand maths at all? Numbers didn't interest him. To an extent, he was interested in history because stories of victories and defeats excited him. He was curious, for instance, why Mahmud of Ghazni had invaded India seventeen times. And he was thrilled by the conquests of Alexander the Great, the strategies of Genghiz Khan and the fall of Napoleon Bonaparte at Waterloo.

He looked forward to the social science classes because of Ms Saraswathi, his first crush. He would gape at her. If he were a dog, his tongue would have hung out till it touched the ground. She was voluptuous, a growing-up boy's dream-come-true. He isn't sure about this, but Ms Saraswathi taught English also... still that didn't arouse his interest in Shakespeare or Charles Dickens. It was comics or paperbacks for him. The first book he ever read was James Hadley Chase's *No Orchids for Miss Blandish*, and he was hooked. Who needed studies when he could read of lovely women like Miss Blandish? He would be glued to the novels of Frederick Forsyth, Ayn Rand, Stephen King and was insane about *Mad* magazine. Sometimes he felt he was Alfred E Neuman, but could never put on a permanent smile like he did.

His parents looked as if they had been saddled with the responsibility of bringing up an extra-terrestrial. The son did not care; he knew what he liked and what he did not. He would jump up instantly on seeing his uncle, Prasad Raju. A grape farmer, the uncle was an outgoing sort of person, and a major film buff. Uncle always wanted company whenever he went to the cinema halls. The boy must have been eight or ten years old when he began accompanying the uncle to see Westerns like *The Good, the Bad and the Ugly*, and the James Bond series. The first 007 film he saw was *Thunderball*. He was hypnotised. There would be a kind of anticipatory excitement before seeing every new Bond film. The thrill was almost sexual, like reaching a climax of pleasure.

Undoubtedly, the uncle was responsible for making the boy into a film junkie. They would bus it to Hyderabad's Sangeet, Tivoli and Plaza cinemas to be awestruck by *Mackenna's Gold, The Guns of Navarone* and *Lost in a Desert*. Every time a character entered, the boy would ask, 'Is he…is he the hero?' He liked heroes, magnified human beings who were plausible…men of flesh, blood and emotions who could exist. Robots from science-fiction blockbusters and superheroes performing death-defying stunts struck him as childish, like fairy tales—not possible.

The boy would watch every film, good or bad, in respectful silence. If someone made a noise, he would get very upset and tell him to shut up. He would get involved in a movie, but never to the extent of identifying with the characters so closely that he would shed tears. That may also be because the boy did not ever cry. Being beaten up by his mother had inured him to pain. He didn't roar with laughter either, except during Peter Sellers' *Pink Panther* which was laugh-out-loud funny. He preferred the slapstick of Laurel and Hardy to the bittersweet comedies of Charlie Chaplin. That's the way the boy was. Laughter and tears were not for him.

In terms of sheer quantity, his Hollywood intake was much higher than the local products. But he did see NT Rama Rao's *Adavi Ramadu* seventeen times—once for its story about a heroic forest officer who saves animals from poachers, and sixteen times for Jaya Prada dropping her sari *pallu*. The film had two rocking ingredients: the hero represented power and Jaya Prada, sex. Ahhhhh, sex! At least in that respect, his instincts were normal. He respected women's sexuality. He would die a thousand deaths, but he would never use abusive language for a woman, although his gang—the Punjagutta street gang—like all others would indulge in eve teasing.

He discovered Hindi movies belatedy, beginning with *Yaadon ki Baarat* and the Amitabh Bachchan movies. Since he believed exclusively in commercial potboiler cinema, he preferred Zeenat Aman's thighs to Guru Dutt's grief. At Uncle Prasad Raju's house, for hours he could listen to whatever kind of music he wanted to on a tape-recorder. He would play '*Piya tu ab to aaja*', '*Mera naam hai Shabnum*' and '*Aaa jaane jaa*' again and again. He would listen to lots of Abba. In Telugu music, Ilaiyaraja was God. Eventually the uncle got himself a more sophisticated music system, and gifted him the tape-recorder. His mother must not have liked it, but he would keep playing the cabaret songs of Helen and Bindu 24x7. His mother did not like anything he did.

Cabaret songs could not play on forever. The boy's grandfather, Venkathapati Raju, chose the boy's line of further education: civil engineering. He had spent his entire life working as a civil engineer for the Andhra Pradesh government. Probably, he hadn't made any money from bribes which most civil engineers do while giving out construction contracts. He thought his grandson could do what he didn't. Perhaps he thought that he would make pots of money by becoming a contractor.

No question of going against grandfather's *firman*. The boy in his mid-teens was enrolled at the VR Vijayawada Engineering College, living in a hostel which was godsent. He could be on his own. When he wanted to, he could hang out with the hostel gang; some of them were rough *goonda*s who made him their hanger-on. He had to accept the membership gratefully. They would not take no for an answer from anyone who had a pair of feet, eyes and hands. With them, he downed his first beer at the age of eighteen. Mother must have smelt it on his breath, miles away in Hyderabad. His father would have probably shrugged, as if to say, 'All boys go through this.' It is an initiation rite.

Vijaywada was quite a town, laid back, but also full of surprises. He saw his first striptease show there; don't laugh, but in a way, he became a man. After years in a haze, he graduated, returned to Hyderabad, found employment as a site engineer at the Krishna Oberoi Hotel which was being constructed on Road No. I, Jubilee Hills. It all sounds very romantic—boy finds job, maybe he'll straighten out his life now. Marry, sire a couple of kids, and reach the post his grandfather once occupied. Nothing of the sort happened. The truth is that the civil engineer was not earning his salary. He was merely counting the number of cement bags and ogling at the cleavages and butts of the female labourers.

Coming-of-age stories have a turning point. He had to move on from those cleavages and butts. He took his first independent decision: he resolved to open a video cassette lending library. His father thought he had gone nuts. 'What about the civil engineering degree? We have spent so much of my hard-earned money to make you an engineer,' the father said solemnly, his voice rising as he said, 'Stop dreaming.' It was back to the construction site on a monthly salary of ₹800 a month, which is what everyone felt he deserved.

He deserved to find a place in the movies. He had seen so many of them, he loved them, he could write scripts, he could direct. He would become a filmmaker, no matter what. Media baron Ramoji Rao's Usha Kiron Movies was making somewhat unusual films then like *Pratighatna* and *Srivariki Prema Lekha*. To catch his attention, the civil engineer wrote an article—with a sensational heading, 'The Ideas that Killed

30 Million People'—for *Newsline,* the newspaper owned by Ramoji Rao at the time. The article about the influence of the German philosopher Friedrich Nietzsche on Hitler became controversial, facilitating an appointment with Ramoji Rao. Sorry, no way. No experience, don't dream about filmmaking. The argument that a director doesn't need experience, he needs clarity of vision and communication skills, was insubstantial.

He would either have to abandon or scale down his dreams. Scaling down, fine; go with the flow and all that, but at the same time he couldn't be complacent. Days chugged on at the hotel construction site till he saw the Priyadarshini videos store near the Lal Bahadur Stadium. The store was packed; business in video cassettes was booming. Idea! He would also operate a video-lending library. That would be a start. He would surely come into contact with people who loved movies. Some of them would surely be from the film industry. Then somehow or the other, he would shift slowly but surely to filmmaking. He would present his case to his father again; he would relent. The father didn't, and even raised his voice, 'Do you want me to rush you to a lunatic asylum? If I have not said anything to you all these years, don't think you can get away with anything.'

Dreams, on that low scale, still had to be pursued. Dreams, dleams, rleams...he slurred on downing whisky at the Madhu Bar. 'Dreams'—just another fucking word. Forget it? Nope, can't. The father's anger notwithstanding, loans varying from ₹1,000 to ₹3,000 were raised from friends and friends' friends, totalling to ₹20,000. That was okay for buying video cassettes...all pirated of course. The done thing then. So in a way, he initiated his career as a video pirate! He was arrested for stocking pirated copies of the Amitabh Bachchan film *Aakhree Raasta*, and had to spend a night in the Punjagutta Jail.

Getting the premises for the video-lending library, Movie House, went on to become another story altogether. It had to be acquired from yet another uncle (long live uncles!) who said, 'Yes, I do have a vacant place, but it's for your father to run a juice shop there when he retires.' The boy spoke against his father's mundane plans, and sought the space for a few months. It was given to him grudgingly for a test-run.

The civil engineer who had given himself a golden handshake would recommend unconventional movies like the Wachowski Brothers' *Bound*. His staff said he stocked films which nobody was interested in. He would buy them because he was taken in by their theme, cover design or synopses on the back cover. Many customers seemed to want horror movies, to watch late at nights. Besides, *The Exorcist* and *Omen*, *Evil Dead* and *Pet Sematary* were always booked up in advance. Since he liked them a lot, he would also promote the Ramsay Brothers' *Do Gaz Zameen ke Neeche*, *Sannata* and *Darwaza*.

He had strategised his video moves cleverly; he came into contact with the top brass of Hyderabad's film business who asked him to recommend what they should see...or not see.

Movie House became a tremendous success, collecting a profit of ₹20,000 every month. That was a big jump from the civil engineer's monthly salary of ₹800 and his father's of ₹1,500 a month.

He had arrived. Those years in Vijayawada meant nothing; those movies at the Sangeeth, Tivoli and Plaza meant everything. This he would never be able to explain to anyone. All that mattered is that his father had never smiled more brightly in his life. P...R...I...D...E was written in capital letters on his eyes; he hugged his son. His mother cooked more sumptuous meals.

The boy had opened the wooden gate of his house.

A pukka Dillliwalli, she has made Mumbai her home. Trained formally in the nuances of theatre and film acting, she was seen in a variety of stage performances, and an impactful enactment in *Oye Lucky, Lucky Oye.* Followed an award-grabbing performance in *Gangs of Wasseypur.* A chameleon of an actress, she altered shades effortlessly as the tough woman gangster in *Fukrey* and has integrated into Bollywood's extended family which rarely welcomes talent from outside the fold.

RICHA CHADDA

Affairs to remember

Blindingly beautiful and irreparably ugly, great opportunities and greater disappointments, kindness and cruelty: any city, anywhere, is a co-existence of antonyms. It's the naïve or the defeatist who complains of urban pressures. Or the inability to deal with matters like autorickshaws with rigged meters, the local train services going awry, the workplace riddled with more politics than a voting ballot-box, and above all, the overpowering disaffection in the air.

No one cares, people breathe their last on the road, the emergency hospital ward doesn't have a bed to spare, a college girl is stabbed again and again by her jilted boyfriend on the staircase of their college. Next: the boy stabs himself again and again with the kitchen knife which he borrowed from his mother's kitchen.

Love stinks, hate is the fast-selling deodorant from the shelves. Accepted and ingested. But is it any different from the small towns which countless people have quit, like the storybook Dick Whittington, to find his or her reason to be? There the bullying, hectoring and the lording over can be infinitely more savage.

Dusk arrives and so does the searing fear of survival. The classic good old angst!

Stop, stop, stop, Neha. That's sounds like a sanctimonious essay. Too many adjectives, too many mundane references. Dick Whittington, for heaven's sake! Deleted, her laptop's screen goes blank. She's attempting to prepare a prefatory note for her application to the Bombay University's PhD faculty. She wants to earn a doctorate in gender equations, a sprawling subject, which she must pare down to a specific angle.

A sociology lecturer in the junior section of mid-rung college, Neha Pandit must extend herself. A Dr before her name would be her late father's wish-come-true. Besides, it would facilitate a more meaningful (and more paying) job than her three-times-a-week lectures at the sociology class which was shrinking by the day. Either the students would drop out to move to MBA courses, or just drop out. On weekends, she'd give tuitions in the English language to schoolkids at their homes. Without exception, the boys and girls would sneak looks at their wrist watches. Education isn't what it used to be. There she goes again, Neha fortyish, statuesque, oh-so-very attractive, draped in exquisite handloom saris, and proud to be single, living with a flatmate in the concrete blocks of Malad. Lokhandwala is way too crowded. Malad's getting crowded. Maybe she'll find a room of her own some day.

A graduate from Delhi University, where she stayed in the hostel, Neha adored her father, a history teacher-cum-principal of a school in Dehra Dun. If it weren't for his pin-stripe suits and tweed jackets, he could be mistaken for an army officer. His pipe exuded the smell of expensive Virginia tobacco. Following his death at the age of sixty-five, Neha settled her resigned-to-her-fate mother in Dehra Dun in a row house, which she visited religiously during the summer and winter college vacations. Then, a lectureship tenure in Pune and eventually, a move to Mumbai where the lights and, she hoped, life would be brighter. Not the type to whine, she was independent, opinionated, but terribly lonely. Her flatmate, Radhika Singh, in her mid-thirties—cosmeticised, voguish and sexy—was employed as a chief copy editor with a fashion magazine.

Neither intruded on the other's everyday beat. They could have been strangers on a train, sharing a coupe. Both respected each other's privacy, but were often piqued, 'Doesn't she care about what I'm going through? At least she could ask me about the terrible day I had at work...not that I would tell her anyway. None of her business.' See that antonym again within the confines of a little flat in a little housing colony.

Neha slammed the laptop shut irritably. If she wanted to do a doctorate, she would have to present her case with more seriousness of purpose. Or she'd get a rejection letter. Or, at best, an indifferent to mediocre supervisor. If Dr S Padmanabhan, the author of several definitive tomes on social topics, took her under his charge, it would be an honour. Hardly likely. She grumbled, 'Damn! Damn! Damn!'

'Damn! That's an unusual word,' she heard Radhika slice the midnight silence. Mercifully, the housing colony went quiet as a tomb, except for the occasional barks of pariah dogs.

'Yes, sorry..."damn" isn't a good word,' Neha said, surprised that her flatmate had caught the slip of her polite tongue. 'It's just that I can't seem to get my application right.'

'So, I notice,' Radhika said sympathetically. 'What's it for anyway? Maybe I can help you.'

'Don't think so,' Neha said with all the politesse she could summon. 'Thanks anyway.'

'What's it for?'

'A PhD thesis.'

'On?'

'Gender issues. Relationships within the urban context, that sort of thing.'

'You mean about failing marriages and live-in relationships?'

'Something like that,' Neha wasn't about to get into details.

Radhika who could be pleasant or drip sarcasm, used a bit of both, stating, 'But what would you know of either? You aren't married, and if you've ever been in a live-in, you've kept it a secret.'

The conversation was getting nowhere till Radhika uncharacteristically volunteered, 'I've been in both. Live-ins are overvalued. Both institutions are calamities, but it's alright, I survived. Tell you what, I'm certain I can be of help.'

'How?'

'Let's talk about it tomorrow.'

Relief.

At a shared breakfast of cereal, tea and toast, Radhika said, 'Neha, I'm no good at applications, but I don't know...I could help you with the editing if you like.'

'I haven't been able to write a thing!'

'See, I've written three little stories about relationships. I'm not sure they're any good. I'm not so sure about showing them to my editor for publication. She can be a bitch. Can you tell me what you think of them? I'll appreciate an honest opinion.'

Neha didn't like the sound of this and said so, 'You want me to be your guinea pig! And I thought you wanted to help me.'

'You're right, Neha. It's just that the stories are about the subject you want to research. Right?'

'Yes and no.'

'It's either yes or no.'

'Yes. I suppose so.'

Radhika gave her two printed sheets, and said, 'They're quite short, won't take you time.' She rushed off, horrified that she might miss her usual train to office to clock in at 10 a.m. Neha's frank feedback on Radhika's return from work would be welcomed.

Surprisingly, Neha found herself reading the stories as soon as Radhika left.

The Blue Frog

The young man had cleaned up the apartment. The young woman's flight was landing at 3 p.m. He hadn't really cleaned up, the mess was just put on hold. She was messy too, but raised a hue and cry whenever he was sloppy, which was very often.

He had been drinking the night away with his male friends. Cigarette stubs littered the parquet flooring. Her CD cases had been used as coasters for the beer bottles. One of the commodes was choked with toilet paper, and still used subsequently. The house stank. There was no drinking water. Or food. The part-time maid had come and left in the morning because the bell went unanswered. He couldn't handle the mess when he was hung over. She wouldn't understand, but he didn't care, not anymore.

However, he did care about the shattered pieces of ceramics which jabbed his feet. The blue ceramic frog—with an idiotic grin—was the first gift he had ever bought for her. He had first seen her in junior college. She was wearing a blue off-shoulder ethnic printed jumpsuit, red hoop danglers, a tiny nose pin and red flip flops. She looked comfortably sexy. Her skin was honey-tobacco. She smelt of mint Twinings because of the flask of tea she carried.

He had courted her with as much affection as any man could. He had gifted her the blue ceramic frog in memory of the blue outfit he had first seen her in, and fallen in love with, or so he imagined. Now the frog was in pieces. He couldn't remember who broke it last night, when or how. But he felt half-bad.

He rarely felt bad about anything. He was never short of money, since he was from a prosperous landed family, owning acres of land, factories and shops around and about Allahabad. He could replace things effortlessly. At times, he had thought, of replacing her too. The thought had disgusted him. How could he? Remember, he had begged her to live with him, in his apartment. Now, since she was doing well for herself as a career woman, she could afford her own place, but had never broached the topic. That would have meant a parting of ways. They had been together for three years. He was twenty-eight, she had just turned thirty. Despite encouragement from his friends and family, he hadn't proposed to her. He wasn't ready, not yet. And yet, he felt pressurised. She wanted marriage, she was waiting for him to formalise their relationship. He had loved her obsessively, but now, it was different.

The bell rang. He hurried to the door. She walked in with a hint of a smile. She left her bag at the door. He didn't help her with her baggage. She assessed the condition of the apartment swiftly. It was awfully disorderly. A sigh escaped her, but she didn't say a word. She moved towards the kitchen for a glass of water. He panicked. There was no water, only some tetrapacks of juice which weren't consumed by the vodkatotallers. They had gone neat. He offered her orange juice. Her phone rang. She hurried away to the living room.

'Hello, yes baby, I am home...I miss you too, you too...I will call you in a bit,' she spoke into the phone. In the past, when her cellphone rang, she paled, assumed a formal tone and seemed secretive. In her guilt, after the call she became more effusive and chatted away as merrily as a magpie. None of that now.

His heart skipped a couple of beats, but he was surprised at how little he felt. She hadn't been on an official trip, but some silly love trip with whoever she was doing at the moment, he was sure. Crude but true. She was cheating on him, the fact had finally sunk in.

She turned around and locked gaze with him. Her eyes were cold, distant, unapologetic. If he could detect some guilt, fear or anger in them, perhaps their relationship could be salvaged. She walked towards the bedroom, her heels crushing the shards of the blue frog. Symbolic! A broken gift, a broken affair.

The young man looked on. Her eyes reminded him of the stuffed deer head which decorated his father's estate home in the village. She went into her room and shut the door. If she had slammed it, he would have felt better. He chucked the orange juice pack in the bin and opened the last bottle of beer.

When she would re-open the door, she would say, 'We need to talk.' She did just that. Both parted amicably. He married a woman his family had selected for him. She was freed from his shackles, but would always remember the glorious moments of togetherness. The first thing she did on splitting from him was to get herself a blue ceramic frog with an idiotic grin.

Everything and everyone is replaceable.

Neha wanted to avoid reading the other two stories, but continued.

Bringing Up Baby

She wiped the corners of the baby's mouth. The house smelled of baby food and wet diapers. For her, it was a reassuring smell. When she returned to work after her delivery, she would miss her child's sweet and sour smell.

Her husband was watching TV as usual. He had changed the channel from the travel show to the IPL match of the day. She hated the IPL. She had always prided herself on her interest in sports. So when cricket became an FMCG, she felt betrayed. She expressed her annoyance with an audible grunt directed towards her husband.

He noticed. He surfed over to the news channel. Neutral territory.

It was his way of saying, 'I care about you, but won't switch to a channel which you like.' A compromise is a must. She wanted to get herself another TV set, but to do that in a nuclear family would be like dividing the kitchen in a joint family. Not done. Sacrilege.

'We have to ask the cook to stay back late today. I can't handle the baby and make dinner in time for you,' she informed him tersely. There was a time when they couldn't afford household help. She worked at office, and cooked and cleaned. But then, she hadn't become a mother. And he didn't have a chauffeur either. But before the baby arrived, they had so much more time for each other. They were happier.

All through her mental monologue, he was in his own world. He hadn't heard her request about the cook at all.

'Uh huh,' he had nodded. In his language, that meant yes, maybe. Not fair. How could he answer an important question like that? She felt anger rising, again.

It had been six years since their marriage. She often wondered if they were approaching the 'seven-year-itch.' They hadn't made love in three months. Initially they had tried, but every time he came close to her, the baby would start howling like an alarm clock. After a few more interrupted encounters, she lost interest. She had read somewhere that the female species was designed for procreation and hence became largely asexual after giving birth. The thought had aggravated her.

'What is uh huh? A yes or a no?' she snapped. He looked surprised, 'Why take your anger out on me, madame?' He gulped down his lemonade, pulled himself up from the couch and walked towards the ribboned cane cradle. The baby had drooled on its apron.

He cleaned the baby's mouth lovingly, wiped his fingers on his jeans. 'If he wants a fight, let's have it now,' she was seething. And then he said gently, 'Dinner is the only time I get to eat your cooking. You're a super cook, you know...even better than my mother.'

That did it. His words made her melt. She was overjoyed. She walked up to him and hugged him, tight—till the baby started crying all over again.

Neha couldn't stop...over to the third story.

Arms And The Woman

The hair on his chest grew in concentric circles. She always noticed that when his chest heaved up and down with his breath. His snores sounded like a cell phone vibrator hidden under the pillow. He was fair of complexion, almost an angrez. *His stubble shone gold in the sunlight which invaded the room through the blinds.*

He turned on his side, with his outstretched hand looking for her. His fingers relaxed as soon as he felt her face near his ear lobe. He touched her below her chin, like one would a cat, and mumbled in his sleep, 'Baby, baby...I love you.'

Less than an hour ago, they had been in the throes of passion. He had kissed her from top to toe, spanked her as if she was a mischievous child and fondled her. She had felt sweat form on her upper lip. Her moans were muffled, she was somewhat accustomed to holding back. She gave of herself fully, but retained a part of herself. Surrender couldn't be total.

Now, his eyelids flickered in his sleep. She knew he would wake up in 10 minutes, 15 at most, light a cigarette and step out into the balcony. Smoke rings would emerge and he would chuckle, the sparkle in his eyes reserved for her. Then the rhythm of the scene would change. He'd speed-dial a restaurant, and order Thai or Chinese. He always ordered more for her than for himself, and would wait patiently for her to finish the meal. She was a slow eater and ate more than he did.

The man had loved and lost. She had been wooed and dumped. All of twenty-six years old, she felt older and wiser than the thirty-year-old baby snuggling in her arms, satisfied with their evening rendezvous.

He didn't read, dozed off during the Spanish film DVD, and had a weakness for iPhone X. Porn would get him into the mood. She thought of the car she needed to buy—hers was too small and too beat-up. Her home needed doing up, her over-fed cat had chewed on all the furniture. He was rich, she was broke. He was regular, she was a gypsy. He spoke of compound interest, she had no PAN card. She thought she was fat, he liked her curves.

Often ,she looked at him and couldn't believe her luck. Not as often, she felt perfectly desirable and popular herself. His personality wasn't in the same league. She worried whether her anxieties would affect their steady romance. Contradictorily, she wasn't apprehensive about being abandoned some day. So many mixed feelings. She fretted about her intensity of love for the man, she had never felt this way before. The cynic in her had been shed like snake-skin. He made her so happy, but she felt tired: what if the affair becomes stale? Ordinary? Clockwork?

She woke up after an hour, her face cradled in his arms. He was watching Finding Nemo *on the tube. 'I've asked for vegetarian for you…and you know something?'*

'What?'

'I love you madly.'

They kissed, made love again with renewed passion, and then sat down to dinner. She was content. The present tense is all that counts. After all, there is no grammar to happiness.

It didn't take long for Neha to read the stories. She liked them to a degree and would say that to Radhika. She wouldn't praise them or pull them down. Her flatmate deserved that courtesy. But Neha couldn't have predicted her conversation with Radhika when she returned from work late evening.

'Did you get the time to read them?' Radhika initiated the discussion straight off, as if she had come home early to receive her verdict.

'Yes, I did. They are interesting.'

'Interesting! What kind of word is that? It says nothing. If you didn't like them just say so, Neha. I'm open to criticism.'

'No one can take criticism, Radhika.'

'That means you didn't like them.'

'I'm not saying that. You're putting words in my mouth.'

'Okay, forget it!'

Neha handed the print-outs to Radhika who pretended to be cool, 'No issues. I just tried out my hand at writing. I'm no good.'

Outside their flat, the housing colony was just about to go into its silent mode. Neha was at her laptop, surfing the net. She realised she was being hard on her flatmate. Forget correctness. She would give her frank opinion on the stories. She told Neha that the stories did offer her some glimpses into relationships she wasn't aware of. Like the role played by television almost as if it was an involved party in a relationship. Another point: the upper hand which males think they possess can be subverted by women who refuse to be taken for granted. The stories were also strong on the female's need for sexual gratification which isn't something to be ashamed about. The concluding story, Neha felt, was the most insightful one, since the age difference between the man and the woman was of no consequence. Men do behave like babies, and women do mother them.

Radhika heard her out, and said, 'Thanks Neha. You're kind.'

'Not really, Radhika. I don't want to be patronising, but I do have some questions. Like, are these stories real? Are they about some people you know?

Radhika replied gladly, 'Of course, they are. But only the basics are real. I've used some fact, some fiction. And the women in all the three stories have something about me in them...I've gone through most of this myself. It's all happened to me.'

'Really. You had a baby?'

'No Neha, but I wish I had.'

'If I may ask, why did you divorce?'

'I wanted a child badly. He didn't. And there were other reasons...'

'Like?'

'Possessiveness, intolerance, mutual dissatisfaction in bed after the initial excitement...there was no way to go on without pretending that he was some sort of stud in bed. He started flirting outrageously, came home late, forgot our wedding anniversary on purpose. My in-laws were with me throughout when he started seeing someone else, they were as upset as I was. I had to quit, Neha. I didn't accept alimony, nothing…it's been quite some time…and I'm still trying to accept that love isn't what it's cracked out to be. Love stinks.'

'Oh, I used that phrase in that note I was preparing.'

'It's a rock song. The J Geils Band I think…that's where I remember it from. "Till the day you die…this thing they call love…it's gonna make you cry." Really corny, but…'

Neha had never caught Radhika crying in the year they had shared the flat. She was no-nonsense, nothing could rattle her. 'That's a front,' Radhika said. 'I'm a weakling. I can't even summon up the nerve to tell my editor that she's under-using me. All that I have to do is edit copies most often written by illiterates.'

'But sub-editing is an art, isn't it? You must be one of the last in the species!

'Absolutely! And I'm working at a place which is devoted to legs, tits and arse.'

'You're doing well…don't knock it, Radhika. But I don't see how you expect them to publish your kind of stories? They don't carry short stories, do they?'

'True, it's just that I'm a stupid optimist,' Radhika rested her case. 'Anyway, *sab chalta hai*. Thanks for reading my stuff, Neha.'

'You're welcome.'

'Will they help you at all in writing your note?'

'No, not really. Not at all.'

Radhika seemed crestfallen for a moment, but quickly whipped out a cellphone, jabbed a number and asked for a slap-up Italian pasta dinner, and gave her a hand-five, 'My treat tonight. And please can we stop treating each other like strangers? I hate that.'

'Thank you, Radhika. Yes, that would be good, but...' Neha stopped abruptly.

'Don't worry, I won't jabber away too much. We'll respect each other's space. If you need me to read your note, I will. If you don't, cool!' and she laughed. 'I'll speak only when spoken to. Deal?'

'Deal.'

Maybe Radhika's anecdotal stories could inspire an accurate, personally experienced pitch for a thesis on gender equations. Even if they did, she wouldn't allow Radhika to read the note. Or tomorrow, Neha would just give up on the idea of a doctorate. Marriages and live-in relationships. Neha couldn't disclose what she had gone through in the name of love. She wouldn't like to share the glimmers of her relationships which were blindingly beautiful as well as irreparably ugly. Those antonyms again. Damn!

The three anecdotal stories by Radhika were hers, born out of her experience. Nothing sensational about them, they were ordinary, limned with moments of pain and pleasure. Something positive had emerged out of the story-reading though. Now the flatmates need not be strangers. A bond, however tenuous, had been established. Tenuous because Neha wasn't likely to open up. She would not disclose her story to anyone. They didn't go with her personality, someone who's serious and sensible.

She couldn't tell Radhika that she had fallen in love with a teacher at her father's school, when she was fourteen or fifteen. The man, as old as her father, lived with his wife and two children on the campus. Neha would brush past him after class, she was thrilled when his hands fell over her shoulder... and then her breasts. They would meet at lonely hill points and at cheap tourist lodges in Mussoorie, posing as father and daughter. This went on for a couple of years till the gossip about a teacher and the principal's daughter reached the campus, perfect material for a small-town scandal. Her father was never the same again, she had shamed him. The teacher was expelled, his children were embarrassed, but his wife forgave him, perhaps because she had no choice.

In Delhi and in Mumbai, her relationships with a series of men were strictly physical. There was no intimacy involved, but she did sense that she was attracted to men who were much older than her, as old as her father. She admired her father: he wasn't even aware of his sculpted physique, good looks, baritone voice, deep... erudition and about the dignified way he carried himself. He was a thing of beauty. This aberration Neha could never explain to herself, except with the simplistic notion that she could only relate to men in whom she saw her father. This was sinful. This was the absurd Electra complex, it happens to others maybe. It couldn't be happening to her. Yet even at this very moment, Neha nursed the thought of striking a physical relationship with the professor who would guide her during her thesis. He would be older than her, wiser and mature, physically and emotionally. She needed the silver-haired, intellectual Dr Padmanabhan in her life. And he did have the reputation of a ladies' man. Just what her middle-age and sexual longings demanded. Someone older, someone superior.

Unlike Radhika, Neha wouldn't be able to articulate such taboo feelings in words. There were no cute gifts like blue ceramic frogs, no wonderful baby smells and no dial-a-vegetarian-dinners in her story. She longed for a father in her lover. It was a sin to even think like that. But that was her, she accepted it, she would not think of right or wrong.

Neha Pandit resolved to write an extremely persuasive argument for her thesis even if she had to sit up all night at the laptop. She did. She mailed it off to the University the next day, certain that she would be accepted. If not the silver-haired Dr Padmanabhan, she would connect with someone on the campus—even if there can be no relationship which is blindingly beautiful and irreparably ugly. Those antonyms again. Damn!

Underestimated for a major part of his career because of his feather-light, peerless style of acting, Raj Kapoor's son began as a child actor in *Mera Naam Joker* before wowing the nation as the lover boy of *Bobby*. A series of romantic successes followed, many of them co-featuring his wife Neetu Singh, as well as a record number of debutante heroines. He moved to direction with *Aa Ab Laut Chalen*, was disappointed by its lukewarm reception, maintained a low work profile before making an indelible impact in a range of roles, in *Do Dooni Char*, *Agneepath*, *Aurangzeb* and *D-Day*. Today, he is as busy zipping from one studio to another, as his superstar son Ranbir Kapoor.

RISHI KAPOOR

Love in the time of telegrams

Romance was another kind of Olympian sport, not like today when it is easier than falling off a log. Today you can pick up a cell phone, call, SMS or email. Letters, I could never write; did not have the talent or the patience. Forget thinking or writing, I could not sit still at a desk. An RK boy was like the roles scripted for him, madly in love, no second thoughts. Automatically, I lived on my impulses.

I come from the 1970s generation which had to deal with 'trunk' calls. Even if I booked a lightning, urgent phone call, the line would be foggy. I would be screaming at the top of my lungs for an extension of time. Not two minutes, 'five minutes, make that ten...did you hear me?' The operator—an indifferent lady nine times out of ten—would butt in constantly and grumble, 'Two minutes over...five minutes over...' as if I wasn't aware of that. 'Yes ma'am, please ma'am, continue the call.'

There would be abrupt disconnections, misunderstandings with the girl I was speaking to, who would grumble later, 'You went off without listening to what I had to say.' The calls would cost a bomb, leave me fretful. Not the cost, just the desperation of it all. The alternative was to send off telegrams. These I could manage. TWO WORDS. STOP. I AM MISSING YOU. STOP. I LOVE YOU. STOP. KISSES. STOP. KISSES KISSES. STOP. LOTS OF KISSES. STOP. I once sent off a telegram which ran into the size of a book—fifteen sheets actually—with its stop stop stops. That was irritating, cost fifteen bombs, but then it was great if and when I received a reply. MISSING YOU TOO. STOP. LOVE. STOP. KISSES. STOP. Not as enthusiastic as I was, but then I would have been satisfied even with MISSING YOU. STOP.

Frankly I can't remember the short forms: missing would be msng, kisses ksses, love lv, a precursor to sms lngo.

Romance via telegrams was a minority sport. Otherwise they foreboded doom—a death or serious illness, or they were glad tidings—birth of a child, arrival of relatives during vacations *(glad tidings?)*, passing examinations with flying colours. There would be silly telegram jokes, too, on the lines of a mamma's boy who after a train journey telegrammed home, HAD SAFE JOURNEY. STOP. GAVE BERTH TO OLD LADY. STOP.

A white or pink folded sheet of paper, delivered by a postal staff, which specialised in such missives, meant bad as well as good news. For me, it was a substitute for a valentine. Not that Valentine's Day was celebrated or even mentioned those days. As for that early 19th-century form of correspondence, said to be delivered by carrier pigeons, were they fact or fiction? Never saw one of those, except in the movies.

A telegram, hundred telegrams didn't sort out my romance with a girl, who was just a day older than me. I loved her insanely. Let me call her Zarine. It just wouldn't be correct to mention her real name. That would be very uncouth of me. Zarine belonged to a—what's the word—landed family? No, an aristocratic family would be more correct. She lived in this spacious, very spacious home on Mumbai's Malabar Hill, with her parents and equally beautiful sister. Unlike today, back in the '70s, there would be a certain amount of snobbery against Hindi movies. Making movies or acting in them wasn't the most respectable thing to do. Zarine and her family were not impressed that I was an actor. *Bobby*, my first film in an adult role, made me a huge star. So what if the story was heroine-centric? From a child actor in *Mera Naam Joker* to a hero, no one expected the transition to be as smooth as it was. In hindsight, I think I must be the only actor who has been a child actor, a hero and then a character actor, like Shirley Temple was. I missed out on life on a college campus. I will never know how it feels to hang out in a college canteen. Instead of adolescence, I experienced stardom.

I am not complaining. It was just that the roulette of life had turned for me. The euphoria was tremendous. Raj Kapoor recovered from his heavy debts. I was a star. I sought to remain grounded, I had not changed at all, especially for Zarine. We would go out on dates to the movies, watching *Camelot* and *Those Magnificent Men in Their Flying Machines* at the Sterling cinema. I guess I was unlike the other boys. I had found popularity. Nothing seemed to matter though because I had become a star, and I was in love. Till a magazine's gossip story threw my life off-balance. I haven't ever told Shobhaa De this, but if *Stardust*—she was the editor of that magazine—hadn't carried a story that I was having an affair with Dimple Kapadia, my life would have been entirely different today.

Zarine had seen the story. She was outraged; she didn't want anything more to do with me. If memory serves me right, I was shooting for *Zehreelay Insaan* in Karnataka, in the fort town of Chitradurg. I went hyper; I kept sending Zarine telegram after telegram to ignore the gossip item. Rumours happen in show business, I tried to convince her, in so many pages and pages of telegrams. Neetu, my co-star, whom I would eventually marry, even helped me write them. She tried to calm me down, saying that all would be fine once I met her back in Mumbai.

Once I was back home, Zarine would not respond to my calls. Accustomed by now, I kept sending more telegrams. The Postmaster General must have been shocked by my obsession for those telegrams. And then I saw her with another guy at the Apollo Bar, the place to go to in those days, at the Taj Mahal Hotel. I was with two friends. I entered the elevator to see her with another guy whom I knew vaguely. She looked through me. I was shattered. They occupied a table. I insisted on one diagonally across hers. I downed Lord-alone-knows how many drinks. I was in a fog. I sent a bottle of champagne across to her table. My mind was spinning out of control. 'I won't let you go,' I kept telling myself. 'If need be, I'll buy this motherfucking hotel right now. I won't let you leave me. I'll kill that guy with you.' The champagne bottle was returned. My friends prevented me from going berserk. She quickly left the place, knowing that I would end up creating a scene.

That was the last I saw of Zarine. I lost her, and it all happened as fast as a telegram. Neetu and I acted in a series of films after that—*Zinda Dil, Raffoochakkar, Khel Khel Mein*. We would be at the studios always. When we weren't, I missed her. She understood me. She understood that I'd gone through rejection in love. She was my shoulder to cry on. She understood that I was a spoilt brat who could spend hundreds and thousands of rupees—a princely sum then—but couldn't tolerate the very idea that someone had actually left me. I would talk my heart out to Neetu, send her flowers and notes for being there for me. We would hang out at the Supper Club, Rendezvous, the Cellar. It was possible to fall in love again. Of course my father did not approve of my heart pangs, reminding me, 'Is this the age for you to go crazy in love? Look after your career first, your heart can wait.'

I waited till Neetu and I were sure we couldn't wait any longer. I married Neetu when I was twenty-nine. Earlier I would have given a peace sign ring to the girl I adored. Neetu, the *pukki Sikhni* that she is, was happier with a gold pendant. Neither Neetu nor I have forgotten my first love story. There's a little footnote to that: Zarine's mother never gave her the telegrams which I would send day after day. She married one of my classmates; they were happy, content, I am sure.

Zarine was beautiful; she still is within my heart and soul. She is no more...she died a few years ago of a terminal illness. Sometimes I wonder—what if she had read those telegrams?

Unmistakably a one-of-a-kind multi-media taskforce, she has inhabited the worlds of radio, playwriting, theatre direction, documentaries, children's films, books and a precious array of films, humane as well as delightfully humorous, right from *Sparsh* and *Chashme Buddoor* to *Katha, Disha* and *Chakachak*. Adept in Hindustani, Marathi, English and French, she speaks in a smattering of all these languages with her clowder of cats.

SAI PARANJPYE

The gigolo

The beach stretched from east to west, merging with the horizon on either side. Kavya stretched out on a turquoise towel spread on the soft, yellow sand, sunning her back. With her hand resting on her folded arms, and her toes stuck in the deep in the sand, she was a picture of contentment. She would have purred had she been a cat.

The striped beach umbrella overhead shyly shifted its circle of shade, no longer covering her. The sun grew really harsh and finally Kavya's back could take no more. She flipped over. Rays reflected from the sea and sand attacked her from all sides. She put on her dark glasses, but squinted nonetheless. The fact was that six months in Paris, *circa* 1982, and she had already severed all ties with the sun.

Kavya raised herself on her elbow and propped her cheek on her palm. A veritable zoo surrounded her. Her dark sunglasses did nothing to subdue the colourful spectacle offered by the people milling around.

These people had come from all over Europe, and perhaps beyond, to spend the month of August on the French Riviera. Having spent a lot to reach this Mecca of *la dolce vita*, everyone was determined to enjoy every moment here. Kavya loved categorising people. Those cute twins had to be Swedish. Where else could such pale blond hair and dazzling blue eyes come from? That fellow with the menacing X-ray eyes would have to be Italian. Had his sideburns been a little longer, they could have qualified for a beard. The fat lady spilling out every which way from her swimsuit was obviously American, reeking of dollars. Every waiter was fawning over her.

Never had Kavya seen so much bare flesh flashed so openly before. And somehow to her Indian eyes, this display did not seem offensive. It blended so naturally with the sun, the sea, the sand. Shapely thighs, rounded bottoms, implanted breasts, dimpled belly buttons, toasted backs—the variety was staggering. Bikinis no bigger than one's palm, revealed rather than concealed. How much would this flimsy bit of fantasy have cost?

The sunbathers lying on the sand reminder her of *papad*s laid out to bake on a sun-drenched terrace back home. All in a desperate bid to attain that ultimate tan—the colour of golden honey. Kavya looked at her own arms. God had blessed her with a readymade tan.

Even the sea was choc-a-block with people. Round swimming caps bobbed up and down with the waves. A burst of laughter caught her attention. It was a mixed group of youngsters. You don't need much to laugh at that age. She suddenly felt a pang of loneliness. Why not march up to them and say, 'Hi, can I join you? I'm all by myself here.'

But of course, she didn't budge from her turquoise island in the sun. She continued to look around.

The shoulder strap of a buxom blonde sitting nearby, slipped from her shoulder, revealing a white strip of untanned skin. A naked little cherub emerged from the sea, and started running towards his parents, basking on the beach. He stumbled, fell and got up laughing. Sand coated his glistening round bottom.

'Mademoiselle,' a deep voice from six feet up startled her. Kavya looked up. A tall young man stood towering over her. He had a profusion of freckles over his arms and torso, as if someone had sprinkled pepper all over him.

'I believe this is yours,' he said proferring a pair of brand-new binoculars. 'You forgot them at the café counter.'

Kavya bit her tongue and smiled sheepishly. Taking the retrieved item, she thanked him in proper French style, '*Une mille fois*.' A million times!

He smiled and shrugged, implying 'no big deal'. Again very French. He then turned right around and headed for the ocean. Kavya stared after him, liking what she saw. Freckles and all. She raised her binocular to her eyes as he entered the water. Just then he turned and Kavya's hand shot down. A second too late. He had seen her. He raised his arm and waved. She waved back.

Holiday time friendships don't take long to develop. Perhaps because the time on hand is limited. The next day they were sitting in the beach café hut across a wooden table.

'What will you have? Beer?'

'A Coke.'

'*Une demie et un* Coca,' he hollered to the waiter, using his hands to punctuate his order. The French can't seem to communicate without gestures. Eloquent hands to reinforce eloquent tongues. The waiter waved his arms about in response and rushed off. He could be recognised as a waiter purely by dint of the logoed napkin he had draped stylishly on his arm. Otherwise he, too, wore swimming trunks, like the rest of his tribe.

Kavya studied the menu.

'What are *frittures?*'

'Tiny little fish straight from the sea on to your plate. Delicious! Try some?'

'No. Not now, thank you. Maybe next time.'

'Next time when? How long are you here?'

'I leave for Paris the day after.'

'Your first trip to Cannes?'

'Yes...and you?'

'I am a local boy. Born and brought up here.'

'Oh! And you are still here in the holiday season? You should go to the mountains.'

'I do. But in winter. To ski! Cannes is wonderful in summer. So many outsiders descend on the place and change its very complexion...you come alone?'

'No. I came with a French family to see the south of France. I teach their little son English. They insisted I come with them. They're spending the day in Nice today. They're really sweet people. So good to me.'

'And why not? Everyone is good to a beautiful girl.'

He looked at her with obvious admiration. Kavya felt self-conscious and changed the subject.

'I really love this beach…it's glorious.'

'Is that right? But do you know the sand here is imported? Every grain is imported from the Sahara. The beaches of Cannes and Nice actually have round black pebbles. This soft sand is brought here every summer, for tourists. For you! It gets washed away in winter.'

Strange! An artificial beach. Imported sand. Was the sea real?

'So what do you do in Paris?'

'Learn French. It's six months now.'

'Incredible! You are so fluent.'

'You really are French. This is the second compliment in five minutes.'

'Right! I'll zip my mouth up.'

'And what do you do?'

'I…er…oh, here come our drinks.'

The waiter arrived bearing the drink tray aloft much in the style of Hanuman balancing the Dronagiri mountain on his flat palm.

He deposited the glasses and turned to the next table.

'So where do you hail from?' he asked her. 'Not Europe for sure.'

'How can you tell?'

'Well, you blushed so prettily when I called you beautiful. European girls don't blush.'

'We are not used to compliments. Our menfolk never praise us.'

'Oh? What do they do?'

'Admire from afar. Sigh. Pine. And when it becomes unbearable, write an anonymous love letter comparing us to the moon.'

'You haven't told me the name of your extraordinary country.'

'India! Couldn't you guess?'

'How? A girl in a beach robe can be from anywhere. Now if you had worn a sari...'

Kavya laughed and twirled ice cubes around in her glass.

'Your eyes are the exact colour of Coca-Cola.'

'Hey, can't we talk of things other than my eyes, my looks...?'

'Right! How about Napoleon's campaigns if you are into history...or global warming? Or better still, you could set me right regarding certain aspects of your country. I have a few questions... We hear that every person does not get two square meals a day in India and yet you strive doggedly to keep barren cows alive. Won't your problem be solved if you turn to beef? Is it humane to keep those skeletal cows alive even when people starve to death? Please enlighten me.'

It was a difficult proposition. How many issues could be touched upon, let alone explained in a matter of 30 minutes? Kavya took a deep breath and began. The childlike and unshakeable faith of the underprivileged masses; the cunning role played by politicians to gain their own ends; the self-serving, lopsided propaganda of the Western media, traditions going back centuries, and finally a dawn of enlightenment being ushered in by the educated and socially motivated youth—Kavya touched on many issues and spoke eloquently and passionately while her new friend listened, enrapt.

Finally, mutually agreeing that India's future was bright, they turned to other topics. Anxious to reach out to each other, they talked without pause. More beer was ordered. More Coca. More ice.

When the last cube of ice in Kavya's glass had melted, she looked at her watch.

'Time to say goodbye.'

'Can we meet again? Please?'

'I'd like to...'

'When?'

'This evening?'

'Er...no. I'm working this evening. How about tomorrow? On the beach?'

'Okay. I'm free after lunch—3 p.m.'

'Great! See you then...oh, what's your name?'

'Kavya...yours?'

'Jean-Pierre.'

The beach bar was totally transformed at night. Gone was the sunny, friendly ambience. Everything was now slicked up for the big dinner dance programme. The vast change was not unlike the vast difference in '*effort*' and '*effet*' seen when dressing up for your lover, as opposed to dressing up for your husband.

Red checked tablecloths had given way to pristine white table linen. Dry floral arrangements dusted with gold powder adorned strategic corners. Waiters now wore smart starched uniforms with shiny brass buttons. Paper lanterns swung low emitting just enough light to be able to see, but not see too much.

Far off on the ocean, luxury liners with their colourful lights made a splendid backdrop. The borderline between land and sea had vanished in the inky night.

Kavya was seated at a table with Monsieur and Madame Peron.

'How was Nice?'

'Formidable! We spent the entire day at Negresco,' Mme Per on rolled her eyes, reliving the delicious memory.

'What a hotel,' sighed her husband.

'The best in Europe, the best in the world. It seems maharajas stayed there for months on end, in the olden days.'

A girl wearing a micro-mini passed their table, accompanied by two young men.

Mme Peron was indignant.

'See that? Why not just wear a swimsuit instead?'

Madame herself was well past the age and shape to sport skimpy apparel.

'Oh, I quite like the mini-*jupe*,' said M Peron in a generous spirit. 'Why not strut your stuff if you have good legs? I for one don't mind seeing them.'

Mme Peron tossed her head. Seeing the displeasure of his wife, M Peron hastened to pronounce, 'One thing is for sure. Nothing compares with Kavya's sari. She stands out in the crowd, like the princess of some exotic land.'

Mme Peron did not seem overly thrilled by this observation. Kavya fidgeted in her chair self-consciously.

And then Jean-Pierre turned up.

He wasn't alone. There was a woman with him. They arrived hand-in-hand. Then halfway, he unclasped his hand and draped his arm around her waist. They headed for the corner table, not noticing Kavya as they passed by.

Kavya stared at the woman long and hard. She seemed quite elderly. This pleased Kavya. Must be some aunt, or the boss' wife whom he was dutifully escorting. Perhaps the boss was out of town. The woman was quite a bizarre fashion plate. Her jet black hair screamed of dye. The layer of make-up on her face had not managed to camouflage her wrinkles, as the layer itself had become pitifully wrinkled. The single studs in the ears sparkled with an innate ferocity—probably solitaires! Age had sagged her bustline, but not her spirit.

'Why don't people act their age?' asked Mme Peron distastefully. 'She thinks she is a teenager.'

'Well she's got herself a handsome young escort in tow,' said her husband and ruefully passed his hand over his balding pate.

The band struck up. Couples took the floor, and began swaying to the music. M Peron politely asked Kavya for the first dance and when she asked to be excused, led his wife to the floor.

Jean-Pierre and his partner, too, joined the dancers. He held her close, and they began to dance expertly. The music became caressing, romantic. The woman rested her head on Jean-Pierre's shoulder. He nuzzled her hair. A shudder raced up Kavya's spine. Could they be...? No, of course not.

The dance ended, the couples returned to their seats. Jean-Pierre passed Kavya's table. This time he saw her, gave her a polite smile of recognition, and passed on. Kavya twirled an ice cube in her Pina Colada. That woman must be sixty. Give or take a few years—actually give, not take. There must be a difference of at least thirty years between them. It was hard to understand, especially if you did not wish to.

Her hosts returned.

'There was quite a crush on the floor.'

'You stepped on my toes twice!'

'Your heel got caught in your gown. What could I do?... Kavya, would you like another Pina Colada?'

'Oh no, thank you M Peron. Actually, I think I am feeling a bit queasy...not used to alcohol. Would you think it would be rude of me if I begged to be excused? Our hotel is just across the road. So...'

The next day, the beach was back to its playful demeanour. Gone were all the signs of the previous night's revelry.

A young man dragged his screaming girlfriend across the sand, to the sea. She dug her heels in, trying to resist. He finally lifted her bodily, swung her across his shoulders and headed for the water purposefully. She howled all the way, 'Help! Help! *Au secours!*'

But no one stirred. No one was expected to.

The young man waded into the sea and was about to toss her in. She clung to him. All eyes turned away as this little episode ended in a passionate embrace.

And then she saw Jean-Pierre. He was skipping down the wooden steps that led from the road to the beach.

Should she talk to him, or just say a dry '*Bonjour*' and turn her face away? But that would mean that she was annoyed. Hurt. Why give him such importance?

Jean-Pierre strode up to her and sat down without any preamble.

'You left early last night.'

'Yes. The Pina Colada didn't agree with me.'

The conversation came to a standstill. Jean-Pierre gathered a fistful of sand and let it run through his fingers. Looking at the cascading stream of sand, he asked, 'You must have been surprised that I didn't stop to talk to you.'

'Not really. You were with someone—what surprised me was that you said that you were busy in the evening. You said you had work!'

'It was quite true,' said Jean-Pierre. 'I did have work. I was on duty.'

Kavya's eyebrows shot up.

Jean-Pierre took another fistful of sand and let it run through his fingers. He then wiped his hand on Kavya's towel and turned resolutely to face her.

'Kavya, do you think I came to dance last night with that lady for my own pleasure? I thought you would be able to put two and two together...I would not have to explain...I am a gigolo.'

Kavya's face remained blank. Despite her modern outlook, at heart she was a middle-class girl, not savvy about the wicked

wicked ways of the West. She had led a sheltered life and had remained fairly protected even in Paris.

'Don't you understand? You really don't?'

He stared at her, trying to gauge her feelings. Then he said softly, 'You really are a babe in the woods. So innocent. Naïve. That's why I find you so appealing...let me try to explain.'

And he did, speaking in a monotone.

'There is a huge section in our society—lonesome women in their early fifties, who do not have a partner of their own,' Jean-Pierre said. 'France is a nation of the young. You are king, as long as you have energy, youth. After that, no one cares a damn about you. You must have seen any number of lonesome old women from the poorer sections of society, sitting on park benches for hours on end. What else can they do? If they do have children or grandchildren, they are in name only, living in their own world. No room for grannies there. If a woman has money, she can prolong her youth a bit. Or at least make believe that she can. She can afford an escort who can take her to concerts, theatre, dances, restaurants...wherever. Obviously this escort has to be young, charming, witty, considerate, handsome...,' Jean-Pierre paused and pre-empting the words on Kavya's lips, said, 'Yes, like me.'

Kavya sat up. This strange young man, so brutally honest, had shaken her to her very foundation. She leaned forward, all ears. 'Life is strange,' said Jean-Pierre. 'I had never remotely dreamt of doing anything like this. I was an assistant in a chemist's shop. Cheerful and friendly, I was popular with the clients. I got pally with a rich widow who was a regular customer. One day, she asked if I would like to go to the ballet with her. Naturally, I said yes. Who gets to see a ballet? What an enchanted evening!

'Plush, soft seats right up front, champagne in the interval and oysters after the show—all paid for of course. I started escorting her around. She would give me costly presents, truly spoil me. And I made her young again. Then she left town, but introduced me to another lonely soul before leaving. Then I started taking money, no hesitations about that...making some excuse—trip to Paris, rehauling the car...whatever. I became thick-skinned. Where was the harm? I was bringing cheer to the dismal evenings of lonely hearts. Every *centime* was well-earned.'

Kavya was dumbfounded. Whoever knew that such problems and anxieties existed? Frisky females of declining years who still craved to cling to youthful follies, required help. By proffering it, Jean-Pierre had the ridiculous notion that he was doing some kind of social service. There were so many problems back home, but Kavya had never come across this particular gem. Who has the time to worry about ageing women and their over-the-hill predilections? Children's education, care of parents, getting a job for the son and groom for the daughter were some priority issues. Our women shift their focus to the grandchildren, when past a certain age. If the family grows, it still grows around them. They are not relegated to some dark, forgotten corner. Tired feet turn to temples. You do not require a young partner to read the scriptures or tales from the Ramayana.

'What are you thinking of?'

'I am pondering on what you have told me. Tell me, what exactly does this "companionship" mean? How far does it go? Where does it stop?'

'There are no rules. It depends...on the persons...the circumstances. But yes, the trail usually leads to the bedroom.'

Despite herself, Kavya shuddered. Jean-Pierre said, 'What's with this holier-than-thou attitude? Sex is ordained by nature, it's a part of life. You Asians make it seem such a big deal. Tell me, if a woman in her forties suddenly loses her husband, what is she to do?'

Kavya laughed inwardly. If Keshavrao suddenly pops off, no one is overly concerned about Savitribai's sex life. She joins some *mahila mandal* or *bhajan* group or maybe some kitty party club. How does one explain this to him—across such a great divide?

Kavya drew figures in the sand with her finger. Jean-Pierre erased her artwork with the sweep of his hand. He said in all earnestness, 'Enough of this subject. Do you hate me? Tell me.'

'No! I don't hate you. I appreciate your honesty. But despite presenting your case so eloquently, I can't bring myself to summon up any sympathy. Not in this, my present birth. For that, I will have to be reborn in Europe.'

'Will I see you again? You will leave for Cannes this evening. But if you let me, I would love to come to Paris to see you. Say yes.'

But Kavya smiled sadly and shook her head.

'Let me be frank too. I will never be able to feel free with you again...never be able to forget that you are a gigolo. If you buy me chocolate, I will wonder which poor old lady paid for it. I'm sorry.'

Jean-Pierre's face betrayed no emotion.

'Right,' he said. 'This must be the shortest courtship of my life. The briefest encounter. If I ever meet an Indian girl again, I will not be so forthcoming.'

Jean-Pierre's mischievous smile had returned. He touched Kavya's cheek and got up. He turned his freckled back to her and without saying, *Au revoir*, headed for the wooden steps.

She stared at his retreating form till he disappeared from view.

The beach around, suddenly seemed to have lost all colour, taking on a drab sepia hue. Kavya straightened her turquoise towel and lay down.

The chartered accountant and management consultant working out of London, dispensed with profits and losses, to become an actor under the guidance of a variety of directors: the iconoclastic BR Ishara, Basu Chatterji as well the gurus of unconventional cinema, Mani Kaul and Govind Nihalani. He found his niche, though, as a director with the widely-adored *Mausam* and *Mr India*. Next: international acclaim for *Bandit Queen*, his bold biopic on Phoolan Devi, was his visa to global projects *Elizabeth*, its sequel *Elizabeth: The Golden Age* and *Four Feathers*. A keen blogger and essayist, his long-nurtured project *Paani* is expected to get on tap shortly.

SHEKHAR KAPUR

Elizabeth and Paul

My dear Kaveri, my daughter Kaveri. You left for India last night, leaving me in NYC. Really missing your laughter.

Luckily I have friends here, with whom I will spend emotional time. Not defined as just being 'truthful' or honest, but going beyond that. Becoming vulnerable. Vulnerability is the essence of a real relationship between people. Vulnerability is the essence of your relationship with yourself, with God, with everyone. Become so vulnerable that you become like water. Accepting of everything. And then let go of everything in its flow.

Here is a story for you:

There was a little girl who fell in love with two pigeons. One was a beautiful white pigeon, and the other, shades of blue, green and grey. She named the white one Elizabeth and the other one Paul. Everyday she would rush back from school just as the shadows of the afternoon were getting softer and longer. Elizabeth and Paul would flutter together and sit on the sill of the bedroom the little girl shared with her younger brother. Not facing the bedroom, but always the backyard of the house. There they would sit in a very regal manner. Facing outward, gently speaking to each other in what the little girl called 'gooterr-goon'.

The little girl was convinced that Elizabeth and Paul came from the kingdom of 'Gooterr-goon' and had lost their way. She would rummage through the storehouse of the kitchen and feed them with any seeds which she could find. Of course being an Indian household, it was full of lentils, grains and seeds of all varieties. So there was no shortage of food for them. Every evening at 4 o'clock, the little girl would start a conversation with Elizabeth and Paul. She would make the guttural sounds of 'gooterr-goon' and they would respond. She was convinced they were trying to tell her something, and if she would learn their language, she could help them.

No amounts of arguments from her parents that the pigeons just came for the food would convince her otherwise. The fact is that when her little brother would try to go 'gooterr-goon' with them, Elizabeth and Paul would fly away. She would show the family the hundreds of pigeons which would fly back to their homes every evening, and ask why only Elizabeth and Paul would come to see her. Soon the family became used to their little daughter going 'gooterr-goon' every evening. A sort of ritual. And the pigeons were accepted as part of the family. They would fly away to wherever pigeons go, and come back the next day at the same time.

Till one day, Elizabeth, the white pigeon, did not come back. Paul would still be there, looking lost and lonely. But not Elizabeth. The little girl would go out and shout at all the pigeons which would fly by and go 'gooterr-goon' as loudly as possible. It was then that the family realised how familiar they had become with the visits of Elizabeth and Paul. As they watched their little girl come back with tears in her eyes because Elizabeth had not come, they would hug her and all would pray that Elizabeth was fine and happy wherever she was.

Then one day, Elizabeth did come back. She looked sad and weak. And when the little girl went 'gooterr-goon' at her, Elizabeth would not respond. To her shock, the little girl understood why. Somebody had shot Elizabeth. The lead pellet from the air gun was still embedded in her throat. Anything that Elizabeth pecked at would just come out of her throat. It was a miracle she was still alive. It was a horrifying sight and the little girl panicked and thought Elizabeth was going to die, and that she had come back asking for help. The whole family was distraught. They all realised how much they too had come to love the pigeons.

The little girl's father was one of Delhi's more famous doctors. Unable to take Elizabeth's suffering, he took her into his operation theatre, and cleaned her wounds. He took out the pellet which some unthinking cruel person had shot her with. To that person it was just a game, a sport. But to Paul, Elizabeth was his companion. To the little girl, her best friend. To the family now, a precious life that needed to saved.

I still remember how my father gently cleaned the wound, and then stitched together Elizabeth's wounds, offering words of comfort to my sister. But because I was a 'man', he would look me in the eyes. His expression told me that there was little chance of Elizabeth surviving. I remember my mother bringing Elizabeth into our prayers every night.

Elizabeth did survive. I watched in wonder as her wound healed, as the wound of a human being would. The family stood around happily on the day Elizabeth could finally eat without the seeds spilling out of her throat. She never got her 'gooterr- goon' quite back, but she was active again and flying as she did before. I have never worked out how my father, a pediatrician, could operate on a pigeon and heal her, but will always remember Elizabeth for bringing such joy to our family.

So dear Kaveri. The grandfather you only remember as a much older man struggling with age, was once the most compassionate doctor I have ever known. That's how your aunt, my sister, once a little girl consumed with fantasies, dreams, love and life, came to terms with the experiences of life. Remember that compassion is the greatest gift of all.

The master filmmaker's oeuvre is incomparable, comprising hundreds of ad films during the 1950s and '60s, an incalculable number of documentaries, pioneering TV serials like *Bharat Ek Khoj* and *Yatra,* topped by formula-shattering feature films. His first film *Ankur* is a benchmark of cinema of social protest, a concern which remained steadfast with *Nishant, Manthan, Susman* and *Antarnaad,* to name just a few. After his trilogy on Muslim women—*Mammo, Sardari Begum* and *Zubeidaa*—the director pursued social commentary with an ironical, tongue-in-cheek style with *Welcome to Sajjanpur* and *Well Done Abba.* His next is a TV series on the making of the Indian Constitution.

SHYAM BENEGAL

Dear Kasim

Kasim: there was no need to ask him his surname. Everyone else called him Chhotu, since he was small-built. I called him Kasim and still do.

He came to Bombay in the mid-1970s from Guntur, a district in Andhra Pradesh, some 270 kilometres from Hyderabad. From a poverty-stricken home, he must have been thirteen or fourteen at most when he joined the ranks of the street kids of Bombay, which he says turned out to be the best years of his life. Without a care in the world, there was plenty to eat from the leftovers discarded at the backdoors of restaurants. He would carry out odd jobs, and blow up whatever he earned at the movies.

The boy found some form of regular employment as a '*baharwalla*' at the tea stall, on the tip of Kennedy Bridge, where my first office was located at Jyoti Studio. '*Baharwalla*' meant that Kasim would deliver tea on order every day in small ribbed glasses to the offices, including mine. He was reed thin and spry then; today he is still lean, doesn't really have any distinctive features but has grown an abundant salt-and-pepper beard. 'Have you discovered Islam now in your old age?' I asked him. 'Why the beard? You haven't even gone for Haj yet.'

Kasim dreamt of working in the movies, not as an actor, he wanted to be involved in the filmmaking process in any which way. I took him on as part of the unit, and he can be seen in my films like *Mandi*, in the scene depicting the construction of a new colony in place of a brothel. Or in *Bhumika* in which he brings in tea and gets shouted at because he comes in the middle of a family quarrel. Apart from such stray appearances, which become mandatory while shooting a film—to rope in members of the units in small roles—he remained a *chai* boy for a number of years, till he graduated to the status of a runner-cum-peon, and then to a light attendant. As it happens in the case of all manual, but key technicians, one had to let him go for better prospects. He joined the technical labour force of a satellite channel.

In between his years with my unit and the channel—during the mid-1980s when he was around 25 years old—Kasim went to his village to get married. A bride had been chosen for him, the *nikaah* performed, and off he went to meet the Collector of Guntur, with his newly-wedded wife. The Collector, it seems, had invited them to tea on learning that he was working with my unit. Apparently, his stock had gone up in the world. He made the Collector chat with me on the telephone, he got a kick out of such sweet little moments.

I regarded Kasim as a friend, someone who shared his life with me. When he returned from Guntur, leaving his wife behind, he faced a situation. The bride wrote him a gushy love letter but he was absolutely uneducated. And he wouldn't trust anyone but me to read that first letter—after their *nikaah* and his return to Bombay. It was written in Urdu, which I would say I am far more fluent with than Hindi. The bride's letter was uncanny for the number of endearments she used—'*mere sartaaj*', '*mere jaaneman*' and '*mere lakhte-jigar*' were just some of them. And the epistle was quite graphic, too, conveying the intensity of her love and passion. She didn't shy away from sending thousands of '*chummas*' either. And when I read out the number of kisses sent to him, he didn't stop me. But he blushed, and averted my eyes when I came to the part of those kisses. Perhaps that's why, he had her subsequent letters read out to him by a friend whom he could also trust–without embarrassment.

The city was crammed with surrogate letter writers in the '70s, busy men with exemplary handwriting, particularly outside the General Post Office, Nana Chowk, around the Gateway of India, and ironically enough outside the University. Migrant workers kept them occupied throughout the day, despatching inland covers or enveloped letters to their villages. Kasim would get his letters written by them, and from what I could gather from his chats with me, he wasn't as regular a letter writer as she was. She would complain that he hadn't written for weeks, sometimes months, at the same time keeping him updated about the news in their village. In every letter, she wouldn't fail to remind him that she missed him every hour and minute of the day. Her constant refrain was that she wanted to join him in Bombay, as soon as he could organise a small place for them to stay in.

When he achieved some semblance of balance in his professional life, he brought his wife to his new home, to the big city in Behrampada. Obviously, I didn't have to read her letters out to him any longer. But he continued to make me his confidant. For a long time, she couldn't conceive a child. Perhaps he had a low sperm count, or perhaps she couldn't conceive. I suggested a check-up at a gynaecologist's clinic. It was diagnosed that she was fine, she could conceive a child.

During their childless years, though, Kasim and his wife adopted a girl child. The girl and her foster mother became extremely attached to each other. Kasim and his wife felt that there was no need of a biological child, since it would come in the way of their love for the adopted girl. Their attitude to life was simple and practical. Kasim, his wife and the girl lived in their little idyllic world, despite such devastating incidents as the 1992-'93 communal riots, which erupted right before their eyes in Behrampada.

Life returned to normal, as it must. Kasim, his wife and daughter would come over to visit me during the festivals—on Diwali, Eid and Dussera. Kasim continued to freelance with units, he had lost touch. Then around the late '90s, I heard that his wife had died suddenly of one of the many illnesses which are rampant in a Bombay slum. The foster daughter couldn't bear the loss, she stopped studying, went into a chronic depression and died a few months later. It was as if she didn't want to live any more after her mother was gone. She crumpled up and was gone, just like that.

After a spell of three to four years, Kasim remarried in Guntur and quickly produced three sons. I asked him, 'Are you sending them to school? Don't place them in the same situation as you landed yourself here.' To that he nodded in a manner which said, 'Yes, you're right.' His wife back in the village makes *agarbattis*, earning ₹100 to ₹150 a day. The kids will go to school. On his part, he still considers his days as a carefree child on the Bombay streets, as the most glorious phase in his life. Like most, he romanticises his struggle. And the story of Kasim ends there.

Except for the fact that the experience of reading a love letter from his newly-wedded wife, did remain with me. I used it as the springboard to dive into the story of a fictional letter writer. A screenplay developed from there, the screenplay of *Welcome to Sajjanpur*. I haven't told Kasim about this. But he must have guessed it for sure. He may be unlettered but he's perceptive.

He wanted to be associated with films, and even gave birth to one.

The well-read and soft-spoken daughter of actor Anil Kapoor, assisted filmmaker Sanjay Leela Bhansali before making her bow as a leading lady in his *Saawariya*. Fashion-savvy, she is regarded as the most well-turned out movie heroine today. Trained in classical dance and acting disciplines, she has been discerning about her selection of projects, performing with chutzpah and grace in *Delhi 6, Aisha, Raanjhanaa,* besides making her presence felt with a cameo in *Bhaag Milkha Bhaag*.

SONAM KAPOOR

Girls' night out

Laura: American, tall, auburn-haired, face freckled lightly, valentine-shaped mouth perfect for a pout.

Charmaine: Australian, lustrous blonde, hour-glass figure, alabaster skin, lips tightly shuttered.

Saloni: Indian, FAT.

Circa 2000, a trio shared a room at an all-girls international boarding school in Singapore. Laura ruled. Charmaine's face always said who-cares-a-damn. Saloni chased away her blues by gorging on chocolate bars, chocolate cookies, chocolate sorbets. She would be scoffed at if she attempted to jog through the school's astro-turf grounds. 'Look, just look at Little Lotta!' the senior girls would cackle like Macbeth's witches. Hubble, bubble, toil and trouble. If they could, they would have stirred her juicy entrails in a cauldron.

And if the fat girl didn't catch the next airplane home, it was for two reasons. One, she would have been sent right back to school from Mumbai's Sahar international terminal. And second, Laura and Charmaine swore that Saloni possessed 'inner beauty', whatever that meant. So would she please stop pigging out puh-lease?

Saloni couldn't. She was miserable, consoling herself frequently with the thought that at least her roommates cared. They didn't treat her as if she was a tub of lard. They were exemplary buddies, not always though. Laura and Saloni scored the highest grades in class. To score higher marks, at an examination, Laura had led Saloni astray, coercing her into writing the wrong answer for what the word '*ibid*' meant—the short form of the Latin word '*ibidem*', used for an endnote or footnote citation; or reference for a source. In her *viva voce* test, Saloni had ended up claiming that it was a Greek mythological figure. Laura had convinced her to give that ridiculous answer at a time when a friend was a faster word-check than Google.

When Saloni wised up, Laura admitted her guilt, apologised profusely. It was just one of those things between girls. Nothing to get your knickers in a bunch about, but next time, Laura would not be consulted before examination hour.

'Babes, I don't know what came over me,' Laura had said penitently. 'I just wanted to be one up on you.'

Saloni had murmured, 'Don't do it ever again or else...'

Charmaine had piped in, 'Or else what Saloni? You'll report her to the cops? Forgive and forget. It's okay. I'll tell you how to get back at her—lose weight!'

Miraculously, Saloni did. Chocolates now crawled in their luxurious boxes like spiders, milk shakes tasted like poisonous porridge and noodles like micro-snakes. Crackers, sugar-free energy bars and an hour's jog became Saloni's obsession. Within three months, she was in shape, not exactly a candidate for a beauty pageant, but not a big blob either.

On her return home to Mumbai for a summer break, her mother was in a state of seismic shock. 'What happened to my dear baby? You look sick. Do they starve you at school? I'm going to complain to your teachers right now...at this very minute. Give me that phone...'

Saloni's father hung on to the phone as if it was a deadly revolver, reasoning, 'Don't be absurd. Our little girl is growing up.' Saloni's kid sister and brother guffawed when she restricted herself to salads, avoided rice and hit the treadmill at the crack of dawn. They cackled, 'Someone wants to become a movie star...someone wants to become a movie star...'

'Shut up!' Saloni snapped, secretly grateful for goofing up on '*ibid*'. 'Yeah, I want to become a movie star. You got a problem with that? Dumbos!'

Mumbai was no longer a blur for Saloni. She saw its seafronts and esplanades in sharper focus, didn't swivel her face away from the slim colonies and the pavement dwellers. Her head no longer buried in the sand like an ostrich's, she understood that if her father wasn't around much, it was because he was a movie star, at the city's studio today, and in London-New York-Chicago for a concert tomorrow. 'Am I seeing life clearly just because I've lost pots of kilos?' she wondered. 'Naah. Maybe I've stopped groaning and moaning.

So come on girl, go for it. Back to school, then your life's anything you want to make of it. The mirror's not being unfair to you after so many years. Smile kiddo, smile.'

The family was pleasantly surprised by the new Saloni, all except of course for her mother who was concerned, worried sick that her baby wasn't eating right. Worse, the vacation over, her darling baby was leaving for another six months. 'Singapore isn't Tihar Jail, Mom. I'll get my degree, come back home for good, and then you'll say, "I'm getting in your hair".' Saloni's mother wept, tear ducts on full blast, when her darling baby was waved off from the visitors' enclosure at the airport. Her sister and brother kept extending their shopping lists till the last wave.

Before leaving for the airport, her father had asked absent-mindedly, 'What's this I hear that you want to become an actress?'

'Of course not, Dad. I wouldn't dream of that. I just don't have the looks.'

'Ha! Who told you that?'

'Dad, you're a sweetheart.'

'I know.'

Before kissing her 'Bye', he had another question, 'Is Singapore an okay place?'

'I guess, yes. Why?'

'What are the boys there like?'

Taken aback, she had replied truthfully, 'Uh, didn't notice them.'

'And keep it that way,' he had made the stentorian announcement, before retreating into his own zone. 'Okay, see you next week. I'll be away at a shoot in Delhi...'

'Dad, it's me who's going...not you.'

'Aah, yes...of course, my sweetheart *baba*. See you after your exams are done. Bye.'

In Mumbai, at junior school the teachers would be uppity with her, looking at her testily as if to say, 'Don't think we are impressed because your father is a film star.' That's why Saloni had felt uncomfortable all through junior school. What kind of inverse snobbery was that!

Never mind, she's fifteen now, adjusted to the nagging feeling of being away from home. Singapore was another world. Even the trees seemed laundered there. As the taxi whizzed her to the school, she felt quite adult. The taxi driver was looking at her through the rear window. She must be attractive, she could feel her high cheek bones, fuller lips. Her dazzling smile razzled the driver whom she tipped generously.

Back in her room, Laura had already arrived, and wolf whistled, 'Salo...nee, you're looking fucking hot. What happened! I want a tan just like yours...' Charmaine strode in an hour later, blasé as ever, 'So wassup guys! What's the goss?' Not that there was much goss on the campus, except for the rumour about the statuesque history school teacher ditching her businessman boyfriend for an IT professional. The girls were cloistered, merely allowing themselves the luxury of bitching the other girls out. They didn't break rules, they were good girls.

That *'ibid'* incident hadn't evaporated entirely. It had left the residue of mistrust. For the graduation examinations, Laura and Saloni mugged away, but separately. At the library, Saloni would take care to sit far away from her friend. No notes were exchanged, conversation was reduced to a quick 'Good morning' or a polite 'Do you think you could turn off the TV, please?' Each one stirred up her own mug of coffee at night. There was no sharing. Saloni wasn't rude, she was merely cautious. As for Charmaine, she wasn't in the pursuit of excellence. She got by and was content with the idea of scraping through. No flying colours for her.

For six months, the outside world didn't exist for Laura or Saloni. They retreated into separate zones. Charmaine was amused, 'Gawd, you bloody bookworms...weird, weird...you're behaving like countries at war...eeee. It's just an examination, not the end of the world! Let's go to the movies...' That was like asking supremely happy prisoners to leave their cells for a couple of hours.

Saloni's mother would call once a week to chime, 'You okay *beta*? I don't want you losing any more weight.'

'But Ma, I'm just controlling my diet. No sugar, no fries.'

'That's so unlike a *hatti katti* Punjabi girl...don't forget, you're one.'

'Ooooof Ma.'

And her father once called, out of the blue, to bellow, 'You got a boyfriend?'

'NO Dad, no, no.'

'Remember, you're only fifteen.'

'But that's the age when Mom fell in love with you, didn't she?'

'No, no, no, she was sixteen.'

'Dad, you're funny.'

'I'm serious. Does this mean you have a boyfriend?'

'No.'

'Swear on me.'

'Swear.'

'Swear *on me*.'

'Swear *on me*.'

'Say, swear *on you, Dad*.'

'Okay, okay, I will, on one condition...that you come to the airport to receive me.'

'When's that?'

'Next Monday, Dad...Mom knows.'

'Next Monday, next Monday...let me see...'

'No see see...you come and I'll swear on you.'

'Okay, done!'

'Swear on you, Dad! No boyfriend! Love you, Dad.'

'Love you lots, *beta*...see you.'

The examination papers were a breeze. Surprisingly Charmaine wasn't rattled, completing the answers before everyone else in the class full of girl students. Three days later, the results were out: Saloni topped, Laura missed tying with her by a whisker of a mark, and Charmaine stood tenth in a crowd of 100. Life's predictable, but beautiful.

Time for friends to part ways. Laura had an exclusive farewell party plan. The three would go on the tiles: drink (alcohol!) like fish, dance madly, puff at menthol cigarettes and cast inviting looks at boys whom they would fob off rudely. Not that they hadn't ever dated boys. Expat kids at the St John's all-boys' school, just a furlong away, were available at the drop of an eyelash. Laura dangled a string of them, the puppets swearing that they would commit suicide if she didn't go steady with them. 'Steady' meant going out on the one permitted weekend to the mall or the movies, holding hands in the dark and promising each other eternal love. Laura didn't go steady with any of the puppets. No suicides were reported either.

Charmaine spoke of an ex-boyfriend back home in Australia. Richard aka Dick—which lent itself to punny jokes—and she were hopelessly in love till one fine morning, Charmaine decided otherwise. She dropped him. He didn't complain. She was a hit with the St John's boys, but would not venture beyond window-shopping at the mall. For a brief while, she nursed a soft spot for Neil, who had spent all the money he had on buying her a faux Louis Vuitton bag. 'It's the thought that counts,' Charmaine had rolled her eyes charitably. End of love story.

Over to Saloni. Subconsciously, she was the perfect Daddy's girl—no male company unless approved by him at some later stage of her life, but she did have a massive crush on the English literature professor, so elegant in his grey suit, blue tie and Oxford necktie. She dreamt about him, in black, beige and olive suits—till that heart-crushing afternoon. After class, he requested her to stay back and wished to know all about India which he had never visited. Her heart somersaulted till he ended the conversation with the pointed assertion, 'My wife and three children are planning a trip to see the Taj Mahal next year.' Love smashed.

Now on the girls' devilish night out, the trio would throw caution to the wind. They would hang out with men, not schoolboys. They would be surely swept off their feet. They would be kissed and caressed by tall dark strangers, according to Laura's instincts. 'How juvenile is that?' Charmaine interrupted. 'Life's not Mills & Boons. Quit your fantasies.' Laura quit twisting her hips. Uncharacteristically, Saloni retorted, 'Chill guys! Let our hair down…just tonight.' She wasn't sure she would, but she felt beautiful. There was an emerging spirit of bravado.

Midnight was curfew time. Like the other students, they had flights to catch back to their different destinations the next afternoon. No issues. From 7 p.m. to midnight, it would be the first and the last evening of its kind in their lives.

Laura wore an animal-print chiffon dress halting alarmingly way before her knees. Her valentine lips were glossed, freckles concealed, a hint of blush-on and auburn hair tossed back over her shoulders. Charmaine abhorred make-up, but helped herself to Laura's kit to look more stunning that she did. A white spaghetti top and a black pair of jeans were her idea of party threads. 'Can't you do better than that?' Laura pouted. Charmaine returned the pout, 'The guys can take me or leave me.' Saloni outfitted herself in a demure, sequined paisley-printed *salwar kameez* with a blood-red *dupatta*.

'What's thaaaaat?' her two friends screeched. 'We're not going to be seen in public with you wearing that.'

'Why? It makes me feel lovely.'

'That you are, babes,' Laura reasoned. 'But it won't do for some serious clubbing.'

Saloni changed into Stress jeans and a black shirt, much too loose for her since it belonged to her chocolate-fudge days.

'Guess that's better than you looking like a chandelier,' reacted Laura. And so, the three girls cabbed it to the Crazy Monkeys nightclub, reaching there on the dot of 7. The place was emptier than a desert.

'Shit! We're too damn early. I'm sure action begins around midnight,' Laura sank into a circular black sofa meant for six.

The steward in a black-and-white suit that made him resemble a penguin, asked politely, 'Girls, you expecting company?'

'You bet!' Laura hissed, and without asking the other two, ordered a bottle of Chantilly to be followed by a round of tequila shots.

The steward nodded agreeably, but said censoriously, 'May I inquire about your age?'

Charmaine had an instant squelcher to that, 'Listen, we'll just take our business elsewhere. We are all eighteen. Take it...'

'...or leave it,' Saloni completed Charmaine's customary sentence.

The steward took it. He signalled the waiter over. Prompt service. The girls sipped the chilled Chantilly thirstily. The club's head waiter-cum-deejay played Elvis Presley just for them. Charmaine was affronted, 'Are they kidding us? That is just sooo vintage…' The waiter was summoned to change the music. It was. Eminem hip hopped in their ears, Charmaine's toes tapped and head moved to the music. Out of sync. Laura wasn't enjoying this at all, 'Let's get out of here. This is depressing.' Saloni agreed. Charmaine disagreed, 'Go Zen, girls. It has to get better than this.' Chantilly done, the three downed their first round of tequila shots. Encore immediately, then yet another. Laura inhaled from a menthol cigarette, Charmaine negotiated with a cigarillo awkwardly. Saloni lit up a Lite, immediately exhaling a thick cumulus cloud.

'Baby, smoke like a lady,' Laura giggled.

'Right,' Saloni counter-giggled. 'Look at yourself, Laura. You're not exactly smoking like Holly Golightly!'

The tequila shots were hitting Saloni and Laura hard. Charmaine, as sober as a magistrate, ordered another round, and wondered, 'Who's going to pay for all this?'

'We all are, honey,' Laura shrugged. Between Saloni and Laura, they could manage a hundred Singapore dollars. Charmaine's credit card would do the trick, 'My dad will freak when he gets the bills, but by then the deed will have been done,' she cackled fiendishly. She commanded crab cakes and lobster canapés from the waiter who was struggling with the music console.

'I don't care if the credit card runs out. We'll just have to wash the dishes, won't we?' Charmaine ordered yet another round. 'I'm paaa…rched, I want more.'

'Stop,' Saloni trembled.

Charmaine, logical as a theorem, said, 'Girls if you haven't noticed, the place is filling up. We're not alone!' Locals and European and American tourists, most of them under thirty, looked as if they had come out of the woodwork.

'What? I can't see anyone hunky. I think…we're alone. Aren't we?' Laura giggled, and outlined the strategy *du soir*. They would befriend some guys, flirt with them and go with the flow. The most attractive targets were two American Navy guys at the bar, in uniform. One had deep dimples and a widow's peak, the other didn't possess either. But the dimpleless one had ocean-blue eyes.

'Jeez,' Laura responded. 'I thought guys in uniform only existed in American World War II movies…umm…but they're so cute. I want both of them.'

Saloni, tipsy, agreed that they were cute, preferring the one without dimples. Too chocolatey and she detested chocolates. Laura needed no cue, she hit the floor and danced solo. Hip hop had stopped stomping from the maze of speakers, retro-rock was on. Jim Morrison purred 'LA Woman Sunday afternoon… drive through your suburbs…into your blues yeah.'

Yup yeah, the mood was lifting. Charmaine joined Laura. They weren't outstanding dancers, but every eye in the club was riveted on them. The American guys were gaping, but they weren't moving…this was getting tedious…but wait, there they go...the sailors had joined Laura and Charmaine. The cute guy with dimples was with Charmaine. Blue Eyes was slow-dancing with Laura. The Morrison beat didn't matter to them. By now the floor was choc-a-block with many more pairs dancing, either glued to each other or flaying their limbs around like windmills.

A short, safari-suited greaseball, who must have been in his fifties asked Saloni for a dance, 'Miss, you are Indian?'

'Yes. Why?'

'I am Indian also. Let us have a good time...let us dance, pretty woman.'

Pretty woman. Yuck. Who said such things nowadays? Saloni's head was buzzing, but she succeeded in saying primly, 'No, thank you.'

'As you wish...pretty woman.'

Saloni teetered to the rest room. Chantilly and the lord knows how many tequilas! She saw Laura and Charmaine conjoined to Dimples and Blue Eyes. Charmaine waved out to her, winked. This was getting scary. What if the intentions of those hunky dudes weren't entirely honorable? Saloni threw up in the toilet commode, brushed her hair, took several deep breaths and returned to the sofa. Charmaine was fiddling with yet another tequila shot. Saloni scanned the dance floor. Laura and the two navy boys were missing.

'Don't worry about Laura,' Charmaine said groggily. 'She can look after herself. She's gone off with Chris and Andy.'

'Chriiiiis and Aaandy! For what?' Saloni froze

'For what do you think?'

Right then, the club went as silent as a mausoleum for Saloni. Jim Morrison lost his voice. Charmaine had said so nonchalantly what Saloni had feared. She couldn't believe her ears. This was unreal. She wouldn't allow it to happen.

'Where have they gone?' Saloni yelped.

'To the Raffles. They wanted me to come along, but American guys...not my scene.'

'You mean they're her scene?'

'Let her find out for herself.'

'Charmaine, we can't let this happen. We have to save her.'

'Save her from what, babes? Love and let love.'

There was no point persuading Charmaine to accompany her. Saloni shot out of Crazy Monkeys like a bullet, instructed the cabby to drive as fast as he could to the hotel. The smart alec leered, 'Where's the fire? I know of a better place, Miss!' Saloni pretended not to hear.

After 15 minutes which seemed like an eternity, she was at the Raffles' reception counter. The lobby was buzzing with international tourists. It seemed as if the day had just begun out there. To her, they all looked extremely cheerful, but what if they were to know what's going on in one of the rooms? Pulling herself together, she demanded to be connected on the house phone to Chris and Andy.

'Do you have their second names, Miss?' A man in a black suit asked imperiously.

'They're American Navy guys...'

'Many Navy guys here.'

'Chris and Andy...Chris and Andy...look them up, please.'

'Sorry. Not possible.'

'Please.'

'Not possible. Now if you don't mind...,' the man shuffled some papers in his hand to look busy.

Saloni was inching towards hysteria, 'You bastard! They've taken my friend with them...she's drunk.'

The man remained stone-faced.

'And if you don't do something right now, I'm going straight to the police.'

The man smiled faintly.

'She's underage!'

The man's jaw dropped. He stopped shuffling the papers, logged into the computer, and quickly located Chris's room number.

'They aren't sharing a room, Miss.'

'I don't care about that...get Chris.'

No one picked up the phone.

'Try Andy's.'

Andy came on the line, and said cheerfully, 'Hi! Andy here.'

'This is Saloni, Laura's friend. Give her the phone.'

'Wish I could Salooonay. Laura's not here. Such a babe. You want to come up? Party?'

'Where's Chris?'

'Probably with Laura somewhere...why?'

'Never mind.'

Saloni knew there was no point pursuing the conversation. She had a hunch that Andy was lying. Didn't she hear a giggle in the background? And another male voice. She was with the boys, so be it. It was the last day of school, the last night of Laura's virginity. Was she a virgin? Not Saloni's problem. She flushed hysteria out of her system, breathed normally. On the cab ride to school, Saloni assured herself, 'No, they wouldn't rape her. She'll probably rape them. She knows how to handle any situation...or does she? Damn damn damn.'

At school, their room lights were off. Charmaine was asleep. So was Laura. WTF? What's going on? Saloni was befuddled, but also relieved. Laura was in one piece. Before Saloni could say a word, Laura whooped up from bed, switched on all the lights and yelled, 'Fooled you!'

Saloni sulked, 'Not funny.'

Charmaine sat up on her bed, and said, 'Jeez, you girls are nuts. What's the big fuss about?'

Saloni synopsised her hysteria at the Raffles. Laura laughed out loud, 'Wow, thanks babes.'

Unamused, Saloni looked Laura in the eye, 'I was praying that you would come to no harm.'

'Naah,' Laura grinned. 'Am just a bit tipsy...and yeah sure, I had a great time with Chris...we walked to the seafront and...'

'And..?'

'Kissed, kissed, kissed and then...the works.'

'You mean you went all the way?'

'Maybe...ha ha...Saloni, you're such a prude. Don't you worry about me.'

'Cool,' Saloni said and was about to brush her teeth for the night.

Charmaine butted in, 'Laura...that wasn't fair. Saloni must have gone insane. You're free to do what you want with whoever you want. But what if you were in Saloni's situation? Would you have behaved differently?'

Silence. Saloni said,'Answer that, Laura.'

'Hey guys,' Laura was about to deliver her minutes for the evening, ' I won't defend or justify myself, Saloni. All I'll say is thank you for your friendship. You care...you're protective about me. Now I know you've actually forgiven me.'

'Forgiven you? For what?' Charmaine squawed.

'Guess!'

Charmaine grunted,'Come on. Out with it.'

'Thank you Saloni for forgiving me...for a complicated four-letter word. You know what it is.'

Saloni pretended to look nonplussed, though she knew exactly what the word was.

'Which word? What are you talking about?"

'Saloni, come on, you're no good at acting. You know that four-letter word.'

'Not really. Do I? Go ahead...tell me.'

Laura spelt the word as slowly as she could,'I.b.i.d!'

Saloni and Laura embraced. Saloni could hear Laura crying. She burst into tears too. Charmaine said sternly,'Jeez. You both are such drama queens.'

The three didn't sleep at all that night. They talked about the careers they would aspire to, the family issues they would circumvent, and the men they would hook...and marry. Love would be compulsory. 'Sex, sure. Why not?' Laura giggled. 'Only before…or after divorce!'

Ten years later, the three friends have lost touch with one another. But they're aware that somewhere in some part of the world, each one has a friend for life. Very briefly, at this very minute their status is:

Laura: Copy editor at a New York publishing house, single and loving it.

Charmaine: Counsellor to teenagers at high schools, Sydney. Married to an investment banker. They have a son and have adopted a daughter.

Saloni: Film scriptwriter, makes documentaries and is engaged to be married next year in Mumbai. She's waiting for Dad to stop asking absent-mindedly, 'So do you have a boyfriend?'

Son of director David Dhawan, he was introduced by Karan Johar in a role brimming with complexities in *Student of the Year*. The film's success turned him into a much-sought-after leading man. Wary of being stereotyped, he will be seen in upcoming projects which take him closer to the league of A-listers.

VARUN DHAWAN

A day before the verdict

October is a killer month, humid, sticky, 34° Centigrade in the shade. Checked the state of the Mumbai weather on the net. Right. It's simmering in the suburbs as well as the city—wonder why the difference of three degrees between the two. The suburbs are steamier. I live with my parents in a Juhu apartment, blessed with the bonus of the ocean right before my eyes. Mumbai people long for a sea view. It's been there for me, a portrait from the window.

Right now, on October 18, 2012, 7 p.m., I've escaped my room for a double espresso. Ebony dark as my mood. The café's air-conditioning, which is usually frosty, is clammy. I'm coming down with a viral, which my mother tells me was once simply called 'fever'. My palms are wet, I'm shivering, my eyes are curtained by a fog. I thought I would be calm and composed on the eve of the release of my first film, but I'm nervous. I console myself that's normal. It would be abnormal to feel on top of the world, or hum 'Que Sera Sera' fatalistically. Not possible. Get real.

Tomorrow is the day of the verdict. And the verdict's up to the rest of the country. I have no doubt that they will like Student of the Year. *But will they like me? That's the question.*

Somehow, I have always been tested at the altar of verdicts. My life was altered dramatically once, when I couldn't quite argue my case before a verdict was passed. Today it all seems so remote though. It must have been some six to seven years ago. When I was eighteen, I fell in love with a girl. Insanely. She was from an orthodox Brahmin family. They wanted to marry off their daughter early. A Punjabi boy from a film family wasn't their idea of an ideal groom. Even today, a prejudice persists that film people have affairs, and lead a depraved life—as if that's a carry-bag of their profession.

Who knows? Together, Nupur (name changed, naturally) and I could have overcome that obstacle, and more. We could have married. I was so much in love that I imagined us sharing a life, till we were sixty-four and much more. Looking at other girls and fantasising about adulterous affairs weren't even an option.

It may sound like a film script from the black-and-white era, but Nupur's father was a heart patient. I spoke to him, pleaded that I was different. He wasn't convinced. 'Everyone thinks he or she is different,' he said.

After weighing all the pros and cons, Nupur and I mutually agreed to break off after four years which just flashed by. Her father couldn't be challenged. I had to make what most movie heroes do—a supreme sacrifice. The moment we broke up, I couldn't breathe.

I'm feeling that way at the café this very moment. Can't breathe. Take deep breaths, look around, that young woman is staring at me as if she recognises me. Tomorrow, she may not. Wait, she's coming over. In her indigo business suit, looks like a corporate executive... she's not. Turns out she's a radio deejay. She wishes me luck, a handshake, a smile...and signs off, 'See you.' Why didn't she say 'soon'? If I was a star, she would have been more effusive. Anyway, nice of her. Need all the wishes I can get. Just 22 hours more to go. Quit counting the hours, stupid. Que sera...that's even more stupid!

After the break-up with Nupur, there was that great big void. Depression set in. Vicariously to an extent, I began to enjoy the gloom. I didn't want to miss out on experiencing heartache.

Nupur got engaged to a guy of her father's choice. I saw her walking into Trident Hotel's lobby with her fiancé. I was about to lose it, go berserk, I was angry—not with the guy or her, but with myself for being at the wrong place at the wrong time. Miraculously, I controlled myself, went back home, skipped dinner that night and derived some pleasure, I think, from the fact that I still cared for her, loved her. I'd get over her, I had to. The show must go on. Next, I ran into them at Privé, a night club. They were facing some problems getting in. I knew the people there, I asked them to let the couple in. Felt cool. Immediately, I went over to a group of girls I didn't know from Adam or Eve, hung out with them, talked at high decibel. Maybe she'd feel jealous. Nupur didn't cast another glance at me.

I was hurting, and bad. Another escape route: Goa. Obviously, I was out of sync with my senses. Or should I say faculties? I did some drugs—marijuana—to forget. No point.

I was calling Nupur desperately, pleading with her parents to let her speak to me just one more time. I was moving backwards.

Her father understood what I was going through. He explained patiently that no father could allow his child to marry anyone without the assurance of security. Love is not enough.

For a while, I escaped to Britain, studied finance at Nottingham University. Didn't work. That's when I thought about acting classes. Perhaps that would be an outlet for my feelings. Perhaps it would remove the cloud of depression hanging over me. Forget a relationship with any other girl, physical or otherwise, I couldn't bear the idea of touching or talking to any other girl. I couldn't stand seeing smiling couples. The rest of the world was happy, I wasn't. How I took pity on myself. My life was over.

I'd zap myself, people get over their loved one's death. No one's dead here, except a part of me. She's okay, she's recovered from the break-up. Life must go on for me as well. My mother sensed what I was going through. She instructed my father and brother to treat me kindly. Dad would laugh it off, though. He's like that, he's never taken any kind of hurdle seriously. Life has sorted itself out for him.

I wasn't a great one for music, but during that phase, I'd keep playing Meat Loaf's 'I'd Do Anything For Love', again and again. Dad would smile, never mock me, he left me alone to deal with my love story.

Dad's not anxious about my will-he-make-it-or-won't-he-tomorrow? situation at all. Everything's clockwork at home. Nothing but the regular cheerful expression from Dad, it's on the same octave. Mum's trying to camouflage her feelings, but she's anxious, even more than I am. She must have sent up a thousand prayers for me.

I'm praying too, without overstating my case, 'God, please bless me if you think I'm a capable actor. If not, I'll accept whatever you think is right for me.' Do you wonder why we remember God only when we are in need?

Suicide! One night, I contemplated slashing my wrists. That would have ended my agony. But I will admit that I love myself too much. I'm untouchable. I love my body, I like to keep it in shape. If I'm so bloody narcissistic, then why can't I even look at other girls? I must have talked rubbish with them because they would walk away, saying, 'You suck!'

A bit mean, that. Unfair. I may not be the most sensitive guy on earth, but I'm okay. I had to get over my first (and last?) love. I had to stop wishing that I was from another family. I wouldn't have had to deal with such hostility from Nupur's father. I had never ever cried before in my life, but here I was, crying like a baby. When I'd see others crying, I felt they were overreacting, getting melodramatic. Understood now, it's natural. If I see anyone crying, I observe the person carefully. I could probably use what I see, as an actor.

Acting replaced, and I will say this frankly, my libido. Atul Mongia and Barry John, my acting gurus, inspired me towards self-analysis. And self-correction. I had to flash back, work out a form of self-therapy within myself.

Nupur was the hottest girl at HR College: slim, hair cascading like a waterfall down her shoulders, eyes which would change colour from grey to a cat's yellow. Beautiful. She didn't look as if she was from this world. It was, but human to fall in love with her, at first sight. As soon as I saw her,

I borrowed a rose from another girl in college, and handed it over to Nupur. She accepted the rose with a smile. I felt like the King of the World.

I didn't know the exact meaning of 'spiritual', but the word danced in my head. There was a spiritual connection, we were meant to be in love. Someone up there had written a script for the two of us. I didn't say this to Nupur, she would have thought I'm weird. I invited her to a preview of Dad's film *Maine Pyar Kyun Kiya*. She wasn't so much into Dad's kind of films. She sat through it quietly. I tried to hold her hands, it didn't happen. She was shy, I wasn't.

Weeks later, the first kiss. On the staircase of my friend's building. It was magic. I felt something else, I didn't want to do anything more, just keep kissing her as long as I could.

She was a south Bombay girl, but never complained about catching the local train to meet up at Juhu's Shiv Sagar restaurant. Our menu never changed: a shared *masala* cheese *dosa*. Or a pizza. Most often, she would pay. We'd walk on the beach for hours. I'd accompany her back at a civilised hour to catch the train back home.

Without a doubt, I was the duffer type. Nupur was the first one to say, 'I love you,' in a voice softer than cotton. I echoed the line, 'I love you.' She said it once, after that I must have said it a thousand times, shouted it out loud. We celebrated the day we had met as if it was New Year's eve. She gifted me a collage of our photographs together. Right from the outset, she had anticipated objections from her father because of my family background and the fact that I am a Punjabi, a different sub-sect from hers. We dreamt of marriage, children. She would take care of me for the rest of my life. 'Let's get married,' I suggested. 'Simple!'

It wasn't. There was no way she could go against her father. 'Why not?' I begged, 'We are not the first to face objections. Let's confront them.'

My love was obsessive. Scary. There is a dark side to me. I'm sure everyone has that. Some of us just don't admit that we do. I could have gone over the edge to preserve our love. Then I saw her eyes which reflected fear, uncertainty. I backtracked.

Her father's verdict was irrevocable. I surrendered. Fighting with him would have been useless, insulting to a dignified gentleman with a social status to maintain. Looking back, I wouldn't agree that Nupur and I were immature. We could have taken on the responsibilities which accompany marriage, age no bar. That's the way I still feel, but that's me. Stubborn about what I believe in, but still open to debate. Individuality is born out of that.

Two espressos down, my love story having unspooled jaggedly in my mind, I can say that acting helped me to move on. There are other destinations besides love. I've taken off my mask. I hope to assume many more different personalities as an actor. I'm at peace with myself.

Hell, then why am I as hot as a furnace? Sweating…anxious… just a few more hours to go. The press show has just concluded, the first public screening will be at 9.30 a.m. tomorrow.

It's another verdict that I have to await. We all do.

Postscript: All's well that ends...well. Now for more Octobers, and for many more days-before of that sweet feeling called anxiety.